THE COMPLETE
FISHERMAN'S FLY

THE COMPLETE
FISHERMAN'S
FLY
The most effective flies from the experts of the world of fly-fishing
Edited by MAX FIELDING
D&C
David and Charles

Text and images originally
published in *Trout & Salmon* and
Trout Fisherman magazines.

A DAVID & CHARLES BOOK

David & Charles is an F+W Publications Inc. company
4700 East Galbraith Road
Cincinnati, OH 45236

First published in the UK in 2007

A catalogue record for this book is available from the British Library.

ISBN-13: 978-0-7153-2546-9 flexi
ISBN-10: 0-7153-2546-9 flexi

Printed in China by Shenzhen Donnelley Printing Co Ltd
for David & Charles
Brunel House Newton Abbot Devon

Commissioning Editor Jane Trollope
Editor Jennifer Fox-Proverbs
Editorial Assistant Emily Rae
Project Editor Max Fielding
Designer Sue Cleave
Production Controller Kelly Smith

Visit our website at www.davidandcharles.co.uk

David & Charles books are available from all good bookshops; alternatively you can contact our Orderline on 0870 9908222 or write to us at FREEPOST EX2 110, D&C Direct, Newton Abbot, TQ12 4ZZ (no stamp required UK only); US customers call 800-289-0963 and Canadian customers call 800-840-5220.

The publishers would like to thank Susan Voss, Leise Cipriano, Katie Valani, Matt Watkins and the rest of the team at Emap Licensing.

Photographic acknowledgments:
Page 124 Andrew Graham-Stewart
Page 132 Russell Symons

Contents

A hatched mayfly and its shuck

The Fisherman's Fly

The fly is an unending source of fascination for fly-fishermen

The search for the perfect fly, the fly that will prove irresistible to any trout or salmon, has been, thus far, in vain. One or two have seemed that way for a brief spell; one or two have proved almost irresistible to fishermen, which is not quite the same thing – fishermen are easier to fool than fish.

While the irresistible fly may be an impossible dream, it is certainly true that some flies are a great deal closer to that dream than others. These are the subject of this book. All the patterns shown here have earned their place among the world's best flies. All are tried and trusted fish-takers for the species and conditions suggested.

You don't need them all. Many good trout fishermen are happy to fish all season using just half-a-dozen patterns and catch as many trout or grayling as the next man. But on different waters, under different conditions and at different times, choosing a fly to suit the occasion is not only likely to be more successful, it is much more satisfying.

It is perfectly possible to stick to just one salmon fly in various sizes without damaging your chances – it might conceivably improve them if thereby your fly spends longer in the water – but how dull.

For most fly fishermen, the thoughtful choosing of a fly from the smörgåsbord of an open fly box is part of the pleasure of fly-fishing: having that choice endorsed by a fish grabbing the fly is perhaps the pinnacle of the sport.

Editor's Choice

Some of the flies on the following pages will be well known to every fisherman. They have earned their reputation over many years – some over a century or so. The March Brown and Greenwell's Glory are old campaigners but as effective as ever on their day. Other patterns are relative newcomers but have shouldered their way to the forefront by sheer bravura performance. The Klinkhamer Special has been around for less than 25 years but is many fishermen's first choice of fly on running water. Some patterns have made the A-list simply because they reach the parts other flies don't reach. The Czech Nymph revolutionized the catching of grayling on deep, fast rivers.

Some patterns have found a place because they address peculiar situations, often when trout are selecting a particular item, perhaps in a particular way. This usually happens on hard-fished waters where the trout or grayling have seen it all before. Well – they may not have seen these. The Parasol Nymph is not so much a pattern as a way of serving it up to the fish, but there are occasions when nothing else will do.

How the flies are arranged

Game fish in fresh water – and the flies used to catch them – are usually divided into two broad categories: migratory species (salmon and sea trout) and non-migratory species (brown trout, rainbow trout and grayling) despite the fact that sea trout and brown trout are genetically the same species. This book is divided along the same lines. Within the section on trout and grayling, there are further divisions into the different types of water: rivers and stillwater.

Some flies could appear in any of the sections. The Black Pennel, for example, in suitable sizes, is regularly used to take salmon and sea trout, as well as trout and grayling in rivers and in lakes. It's an excellent all-round fly. It appears in the section on flies for wild brown trout in natural lakes. That's where it is most commonly employed but it would not be out of place on any water. Similarly, the Endrick Spider was originally created to catch salmon and sea trout; so it does – but it excels as a general pattern for trout and grayling in rivers and so that is where you'll find it.

The sections are only meant as a guide to where each fly is used. Most patterns can be – and are – used everywhere.

You will not find every fly here – but you will find every fly you will ever need.

STEP-BY-STEP FLY-TYING GUIDES

Fishing folk have been arguing about the fly invented by the Macedonian fisherman Hippouros since it was first described by Claudius Aelianus around AD200:

> *...fasten red wool around the hook, and fix on to the wool two feathers which grow under a cock's wattles and which in colour are like wax.*

Did this mean hackles? And were they wound round the length of the body, palmer-style, or tied in as wings?

Every fly in this book (except the Hippouros) is accompanied by a photograph and formula. Unless a variation is mentioned this will be the original tying of the fly or the usually accepted version. If the pattern is not readily available in tackle shops or mail-order catalogues there will be a step-by-step guide to tying the pattern. These step-by-step guides illustrate any unusual techniques or tying sequences, or a reference at the bottom of the page will take you to a previous example.

The dressings of some famous flies have been so abused and adulterated over the years that what can be offered for sale now has little more than the name in common with the original pattern – and in the case of the Klinkhamer Special even that may be only approximate. In these cases, a step-by-step guide shows the authentic tying sequence.

Scale

For the purposes of showing detail, The flies shown in the step-by-step sequences are illustrated larger than actual size and their relative proportions vary.

Trout and

Grayling

Resident trout and grayling get all their food from the water around them, usually as insects in various stages, but also as other things that live in the water (fish fry, water snails, crayfish and other creatures) or have otherwise ended up in it (mice, sliced bread and so on). It is usually presumed that the fisherman's fly is taken in mistake for one of these. Flies have been tied to imitate all of these things, including the sliced bread, and they catch fish.

Trout and grayling will, of course, also take flies that look nothing remotely like any sort of food. Why is a mystery, but it is one of the charms of fly-fishing that the fish will occasionally refute the angler's most cherished theories. There has always been a role for whim in the creation of successful flies.

Most trout and grayling flies are imitations of trout and grayling food but, perversely, flies that offer a general impression of an insect often do better than an exact copy, perfect in every detail. This is a source of great comfort to those of us without the patience or dexterity to tie perfect imitations or the cash to buy them.

The Macedonian fishermen (see page 9) used an artificial fly when the fish in their streams were gorging on a natural fly: 'in size you might call it a midge, it imitates the colour of a wasp'. But the Macedonian fishermen tied their flies with red wool – presumably because that worked.

The most successful patterns are usually a mixture of imitation and whim but, however they were dreamed up, all the angler's creations are subject to the final judgment of the fish.

Rivers and Streams

Brown trout and grayling both need cool, well-oxygenated water in which to spawn and feed

Trout and grayling make their living from the creatures that share their habitat. Flies that imitate those creatures will take both trout and grayling, and any pattern in this section can be used for either species. They may not work equally well. When trout and grayling live in the same river, the grayling tend to inhabit the depths, sheltering in the hollows of the bottom below the main current. Trout are more likely to be found at the edges of the current and the margins of the river. Flies that work in the depths of fast rivers must be heavy and slim to sink as quickly as possible. These are the archetypal grayling flies, developed by Polish and Czech competition fishermen to winkle grayling out from previously inaccessible lies at the bottom of large, swift rivers. They are, of course, just as acceptable to any trout in the vicinity. There has long been a tradition that flies cast for grayling should have a touch of red about their person, a red tag or a red tail in the dressing. The pattern described on page 20 offers a possible explanation for this.

Many of the insects and other organisms in rivers and streams can also be found in stillwaters or have stillwater relatives that look much the same. Adult caddis (sedge) imitations work equally well on lake or stream, twitched across the surface when the naturals are hatching of a summer's evening. But many river patterns need the movement of a current to perform their magic. Slim, spider patterns are indifferent performers on a loch or reservoir but they are deadly in the bouncing current of a rocky, rain-fed river.

Trout and, to a lesser extent, grayling take up permanent lies in running water. In clear water they can been seen for days, sometimes weeks and seasons, in the same spot. Even when the fish are invisible they lie in predictable places or a rise will betray their location. Fishermen notice these things. On a well-fished stream these fish will see a lot of flies: they can become very good at sorting fact from fiction. This may explain why the flies in this section tend to be closer imitations of natural insects than those used on stillwaters.

The patterns are ordered by the usual depth of presentation, from bottom-bouncing nymphs to high-riding dry-flies.

Bouncing the Bottom

Imitating the case-building caddis larvae that trundle the river bed

The most easily recognized type of sedge (caddis) larva is one that builds itself a protective case using a variety of materials, from sand and small stones to tiny shells and plant material. Some, like the larvae of the great red sedge, cut a length of reed into a strip and wrap it around their bodies to form a long, tapered case.

Trout and grayling are quite partial to feeding on cased caddis larvae, particularly through the winter and into early spring when there may be little else to eat. The fish will swallow the larvae, case and all. This is fortunate for the angler because it allows a large, quick-sinking fly to be used, but one that still imitates a natural food item.

Patterns such as the Peeping Caddis are perfect examples of this type of fly, for when tied with a

PEEPING CADDIS

HOOK: Size 8–12 longshank

UNDERBODY: Medium lead wire

HEAD: Black or gold 3–4mm metal bead, tungsten if possible

THREAD: Brown

TAIL: Cream or light green yarn (not wool)

BODY: Brown sparkle yarn or dark hare's fur, dubbed

HACKLE: Brown partridge hackle

TYING THE PEEPING CADDIS

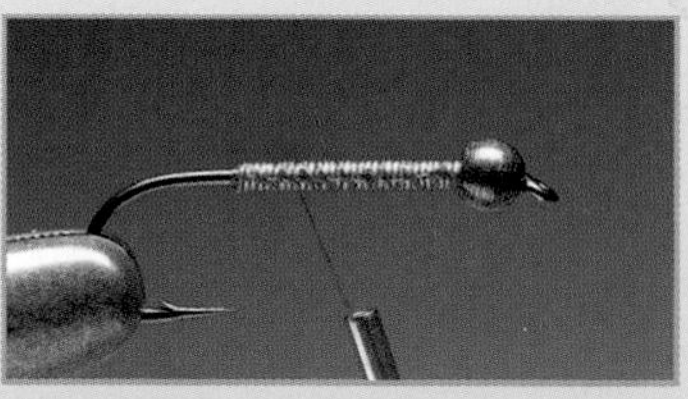

1 Slip on a 3–4mm metal bead, either gold or black, before mounting the hook. Wind medium-width lead wire down the shank in close turns. Push the wire up into the recess at the base of the bead, leaving a short section of shank bare at the rear. Secure the lead wire in place with tying thread.

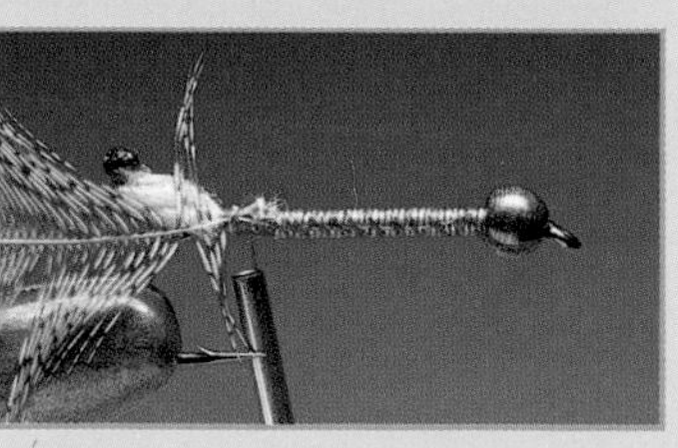

2 Wind the hackle in touching turns.

3 Wind on two full turns. Stroke the fibres towards the hook bend as each turn is made. Secure and trim. Make a few turns of thread at the base of the hackle, keeping the fibres pointing over the head.

4 Tease out the fibres of some brown sparkle yarn. Dub on to the tying thread to form a thick rope. Wind the dubbed yarn towards the bead in close turns, right up to the base of the bead. Allowing the dubbing to spread from halfway along produces a slight taper to the body. Cast off the tying thread with a whip finish.

RELATED SUBJECTS: • Czech nymphing p16 • Weighting flies p24 • Fixing beads p25

heavy, lead underbody they sink very quickly, allowing them to be bumped slowly along the riverbed even in fast water.

The Peeping Caddis is designed to imitate a cased sedge larva as it trundles along the riverbed. Often its body and legs will protrude well out of its case and it is this aspect that Oliver Edwards' pattern imitates so well. By using a short length of pale yarn, singed to create a dark blob at one end, a simple but extremely lifelike impression of the body and head are created. The addition of long fibres from a partridge hackle completes the illusion, representing the insect's legs and also adding some mobility to the fly.

As the Peeping Caddis is designed to fish right on the riverbed, it is heavily weighted with close turns of lead wire and, in the original, a split shot connected near the eye of the hook by a loop of nylon. In this version a metal bead, slipped along the shank, replaces the split shot.

Tied with all this weight, the finished pattern sinks very quickly and also sits with the hook point slightly raised, helping to prevent it from snagging the bottom.

tips

- Works best in deeper pools and runs, especially where there is a good flow rate. Especially good for winkling out a fish from a deep pocket.
- Fished either singly or as the point fly with another nymph on the dropper. It should be cast well upstream to allow it plenty of time to sink to the bottom, especially when fishing deeper stretches. It should then be allowed to bump along the riverbed until it has drifted downstream of the angler.

A cased caddis larva

Riverbed Revolution

A caddis without a case, and the nymph that changed grayling fishing for ever

While all sedge larvae construct cases in which to pupate, not all live in them permanently. A number spend their lives prior to this stage swimming freely. Two main groups of sedges have free-swimming larvae; these are the *Hydropsyche* and the *Rhyacophila*. As well as being caseless, Hydropsyche larvae build webs in which they collect their food, and when the river is running clear these can be seen quite clearly dotted around beds of weed.

The two types are easily distinguished: Rhyacophila larvae are generally a pale, translucent green while those of the Hydropsyche are pale brown and noticeably darker around the head and thorax region. Both are free-swimming and can form a large part of the grayling's diet. Trout take them just as readily. The Hydropsyche larva is the model for the renowned Czech Nymph. This imitation can be very heavily weighted and its slim profile helps it sink quickly to the grayling's feeding zone.

The Czech Nymph

This is the ultimate grayling fly, born on the big, fast rivers of eastern Europe where the grayling is king.

When first introduced by Czech and Polish anglers, this pattern revolutionized grayling fishing in the rest of the world, particularly on fast, rain-fed rivers. Here was a pattern that was so heavily weighted that it could be bumped along the river-bed even in fast-flowing water – just where the grayling were sitting.

The pattern brought with it a new technique. Though a single fly may be used, the favoured technique is to use a team of two or three similar patterns. The nymphs are fished at short range, almost under the rod tip. The team is cast a short way upstream and the drift downstream is followed by the rod-top. The line hangs vertically and should be watched carefully for signs of a take. These usually manifest themselves by a pause or deviation in the natural drift of the line rather than a pull that can be felt; any such movement should be met with a firm but steady lift of the rod.

CZECH NYMPH

HOOK: Size 8–12 heavyweight grub hook
THREAD: Brown
MAIN RIB: Clear nylon monofilament
SHELL-BACK: Tan plastic strip
BODY RIB: Fine, flat gold tinsel
BODY: Amber or tan fur dubbing
HOT SPOT: Green dubbing
THORAX: Hare's fur

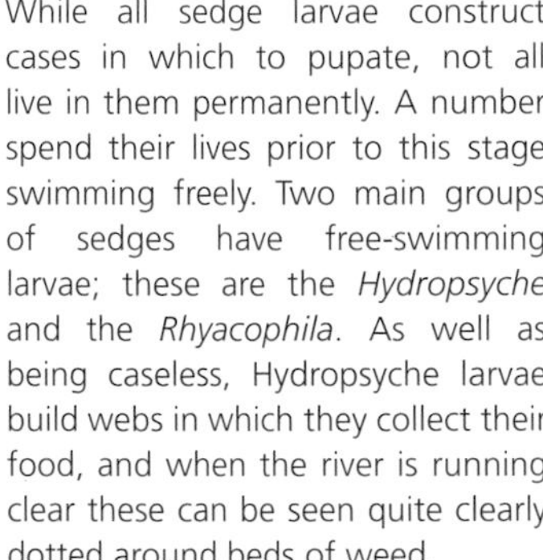

Hydropsyche larva

RELATED SUBJECT: • Weighting flies p24

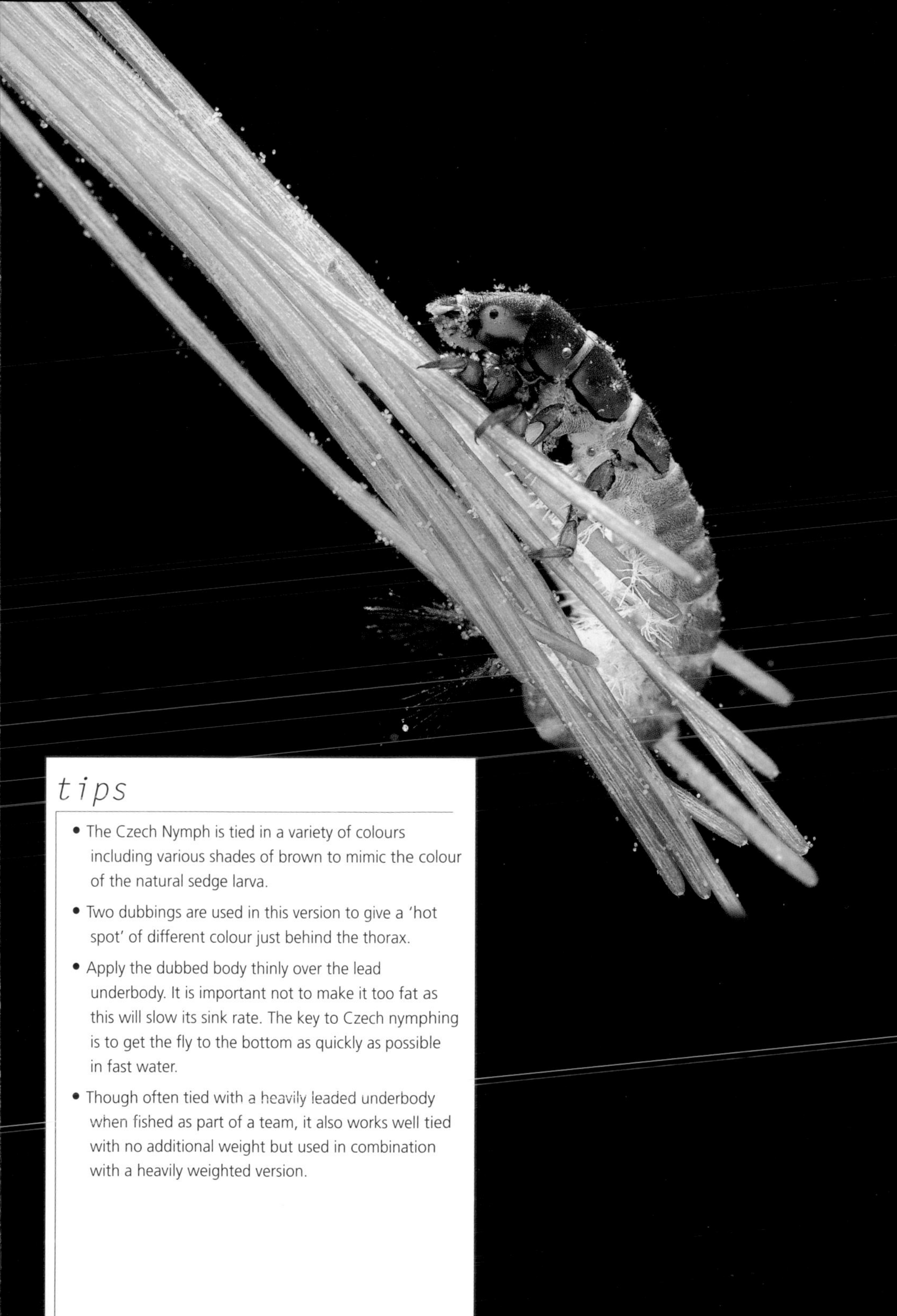

tips

- The Czech Nymph is tied in a variety of colours including various shades of brown to mimic the colour of the natural sedge larva.
- Two dubbings are used in this version to give a 'hot spot' of different colour just behind the thorax.
- Apply the dubbed body thinly over the lead underbody. It is important not to make it too fat as this will slow its sink rate. The key to Czech nymphing is to get the fly to the bottom as quickly as possible in fast water.
- Though often tied with a heavily leaded underbody when fished as part of a team, it also works well tied with no additional weight but used in combination with a heavily weighted version.

Branko's Brainchild

Lively nymphs for deep waters

The Slovenian fly-dresser Branko Gasparin is known for his innovation. He has a relaxed tying manner that is misleading. As he chats, nothing much seems to be happening but then, following a blur of fingers, another creation leaves his vice. Branko ties 8,000 flies per season.

With the Soca and many other pristine rivers on his doorstep, Branko has an enviable opportunity to study fish behaviour almost daily. Despite the Soca being ranked as the better river by many, Branko's favourite is the Idrijca, where the topography gives more opportunities to study the habits of fish. From this, Branko has gleaned an in-depth understanding of his quarry, which is reflected in his fly-tying.

A common theme – the inclusion of foam – runs through nearly all his nymph dressings. The reason is simple. Slovenia has a single-fly policy throughout its regions. For single flies to sink sufficiently deeply, and quickly, to find the dark chasms that harbour huge trout, hooks need loading with considerable ballast. This is fine when fishing nymphs are

BRANKO NYMPH
HOOK: **Size 10–14**
THREAD: **Tan**
ABDOMEN: **Beige foam**
RIB: **Red floss**
THORAX: **Natural hare or squirrel fur**
HACKLE: **Natural grey CDC**

TYING THE BRANKO NYMPH

1 Run on the tying thread immediately behind the eye then catch in a length of red floss plus a strip of foam.

2 Using touching turns of thread, secure the foam and floss along the full length of the hook shank.

3 Return the thread to a position one third of the way from the hook, then wind the foam strip to form a tapered abdomen.

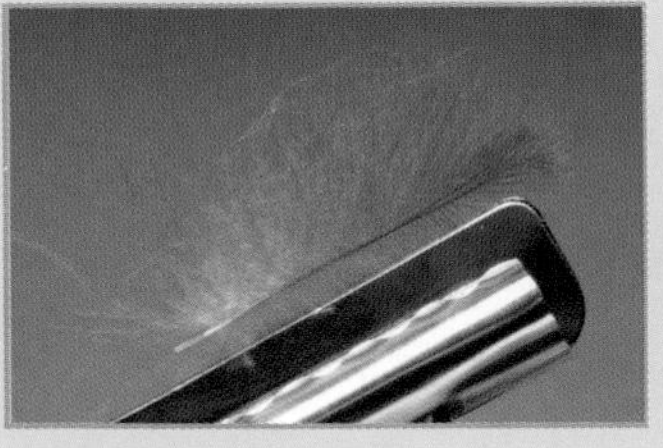

7 Prepare the CDC feathers by placing a couple of plumes in a Marc Petitjean transparent clip or bulldog clip.

8 Spin the bobbin-holder in an anticlockwise direction to flatten the thread. Using a fine dubbing needle, split the thread lengthways to creating a 'refined' dubbing loop.

9 Carefully cut away the feather stalk from the CDC feathers before introducing the fibres into the gap formed in the split thread.

RELATED SUBJECT: • Czech nymphing p16

tied on large hooks – but, even when weighted to the hilt, a size 16 fly just flutters pathetically in the heavy Slovenian waters. Furthermore, if these flies ever found the mark, with so many lead wraps restricting the gape of the hook, one would have to rely on a large slice of luck to hook a trout. The solution is a non-toxic split shot connected to the leader a little way up from the fly, a recognized tactic in the United States and Europe. Thus, the same fly may be used to search a range of depths by simply adding or removing shot where necessary.

Exploring this further, Branko realized that unweighted nymphs, reliant on the shot to take them down, behaved more naturally than those with the weight in the dressing. By incorporating foam into many of his nymphs, Branko achieved a degree of buoyancy. Cut into strips, the foam (nothing expensive, it is merely packing foam) can be wound like any other material to create attractive soft bodies. Because it is perhaps not as buoyant as, say, Ethafoam or Plastazote, the flies hover in the current above the rocky bottom. During the course of a day these foam-bodied nymphs can become a little saturated, though a quick squeeze between the fingers expels any excess moisture and puts you back in business. This ingenious concept conjures up all kinds of ideas for deep, mobile nymphs.

Where split shot weights are frowned upon, a large, heavy nymph (a sacrificial fly) can be tied on a dropper, allowing a foam creation to move freely on the point.

tip

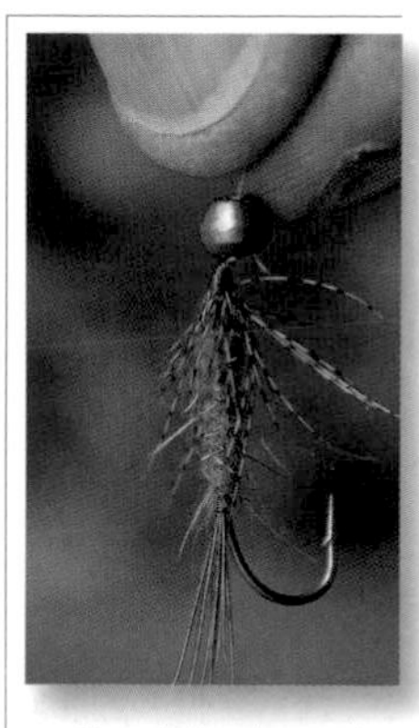

- Unweighted nymphs can be turned into depth-seekers by slipping a metal bead on to the tippet before tying

4 Take care not to wind the foam so tightly as to compress and destroy its buoyancy. Secure the loose end of foam and cut away waste.

5 Take hold of the red floss and wind it carefully over the foam abdomen using open, evenly spaced turns to form the rib.

6 Dub on a small amount of hare or squirrel fur to form a thorax, winding back from the eye.

10 Remove the bulldog clip then spin the bobbin-holder in a clockwise direction to trap and flare the CDC.

11 Wind the CDC fibres towards the eye, in touching turns. Stroke the CDC fibres so they lie back over the body like a conventional hackle.

12 Form a neat head and complete the fly with a four-turn whip finish.

Spot the Difference

Scientific research and the birth of a deadly shrimp imitation

About 20 years ago Neil Patterson first drew fly-fishers' attention to the small orangey-red spot on the backs of some shrimps. He devised his Red-Spot Shrimp as an imitation, and it worked pretty well.

More recently, three scientists from the University of Berne in Switzerland discovered that the orange spot is a parasite – a spiny-headed worm (*Pomphorhynchus laevis*). The parasite causes the shrimp to be less sensitive to light. The result is that, rather than remaining in their favoured darker habitats in a weed bed or under stones, the shrimps swim in open water: their behaviour alters to expose them to predation.

These parasites are devious creatures because they de-sensitize the shrimp for a specific purpose. They want the shrimp to be eaten by a fish so that the parasite can enter its final host. In the research (published in *Ecology*), the final host was the male stickleback. The parasite is an important source of carotene, used by the male stickleback to develop its bright orangey-red breeding colours. Grayling or trout may take them for a similar reason: at the time of spawning the large reddish dorsal fin of the male grayling is more brightly coloured than during the rest of the year.

The researchers from Berne University were able to prove that male sticklebacks actively selected infected orange-spot shrimps. Do grayling do the same? If they do, does it at last provide an answer to why grayling flies with a touch of red, orange or yellow have proved so successful, especially in the autumn and winter period immediately prior to spawning?

John Roberts improved on Neil Patterson's original. He tied weighted shrimps with an orange bead in the middle of the body. They are bright and draw attention to themselves in the fly box, even among the array of gold, copper, silver and black-headed bugs and nymphs. The plastic bead doesn't reflect light as the metal ones do, but the fluorescent orange is brighter and easier to see in the water than any gold head.

'My first chance to try out the pattern was on a visit to the Wiltshire Avon for grayling. On my first cast I had a take as the Shrimp sank. Within a minute or two I had accustomed myself to the speed of the grayling takes and landed my first fish on the new fly. By late afternoon I reckon I had caught more than 80 grayling on this one pattern.'

Fish the fly in a dead drift, but if the takes are too quick to react to, you must retrieve the Shrimp faster than the current. This commits the grayling to a firmer take, a faster interception or often a downstream follow, and should make hooking a lot easier.

ORANGE-SPOT SHRIMP

HOOK: Partridge K4A size 12

THREAD: Tan

UNDERBODY: Two small mounds of wound lead or copper wire

BEAD: 3mm fluorescent orange plastic bead

BODY: Tan Fly Rite Poly Seal (Niche Products)

BACK: Clear polythene strip

RIB: Fine copper wire

RELATED SUBJECT:
• Using plastics p94

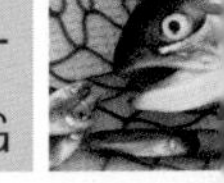

tips

- What anglers call freshwater shrimps (*Gammarus*) are not true shrimps at all but belong to the order Amphipoda. They are crustaceans and are available to the fish throughout the year. They are to be found in both lakes and rivers, though they prefer a rich, alkaline environment and are less numerous in acidic waters. Shrimp imitations work best when fished close to the bottom, where the naturals are most often found.
- The shrimp is normally fished dead-drift, cast upstream of a likely looking spot and allowed to drift back at the same speed as the current. In clear water its visibility makes it a great fly for targeting specimen grayling where an individual fish can easily be seen taking the pattern.

Freshwater shrimp

• Fishing with combinations of flies p104

Bugs and Beads

Wire and beads are used to adapt any nymph pattern to fish deeper

Flies designed for the middle layers of a river will all carry some sort of weight. How much will depend on the speed of the current, the profile of the fly and whether it is to be fished upstream or downstream, singly or in a team (where the combined weight of the team can be used to get the flies deeper than a single fly). This is the region of bugs and beads.

To cover most situations the angler carries flies in a variety of weights. Each will have an underbody of lead or copper wire or incorporate a metal bead (brass, copper or tungsten) in the dressing. The bead itself attracts the attention of the fish: it is said to imitate the bubble of air that some species, particularly caddis pupae, use to ascend towards the surface.

A vast array of patterns can be created by adding beads of varying weight and colour to any proven nymph pattern. There can be few river fishermen who have not taken

BEAD SAWYER BUG

- HOOK: Size 10–14 wet-fly
- THREAD: Beige
- TAIL: Fluorescent orange floss
- RIB: Fine copper wire
- BODY: Beige or grey wool
- HEAD: 2–3mm gold, silver or copper bead

TYING THE BEAD SAWYER BUG

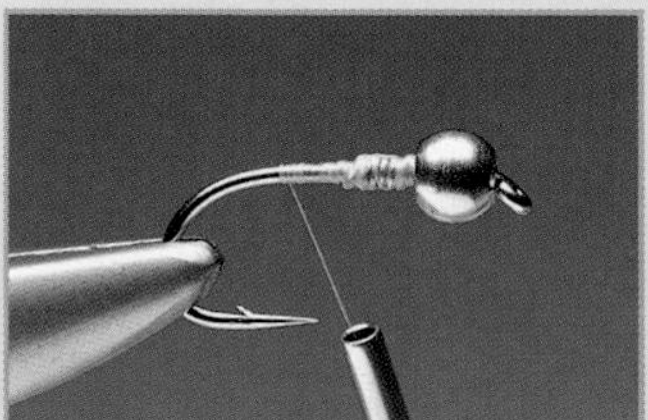

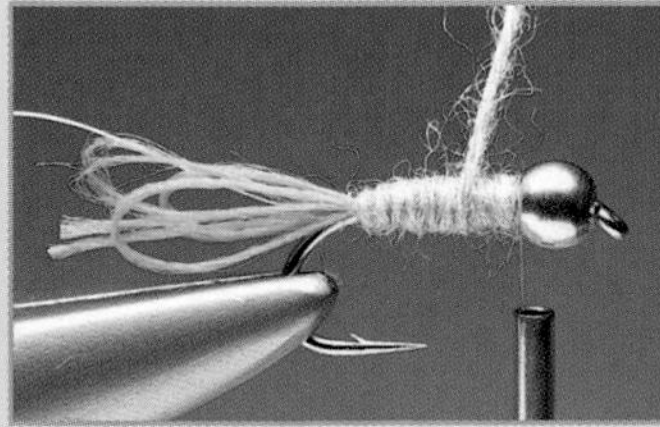

1 Slip a 3–4mm gold bead over the hook point. Push the gold bead right up to the eye. Take 2in of fine lead wire and wind 10–15 close turns along the shank of the hook. Push it into the recess at the back of the bead and fix the wire in place with turns of tying thread.

2 Carry the tying thread down to the bend then take a length of fluorescent orange floss and double it over four times to form eight strands. Tie it in at the bend to form the tail, using the waste ends to fill the gap up to the lead underbody. Catch in 2in of fine copper wire at the tail.

3 Take 3in of fine, beige wool and catch it in with the thread behind the bead. Wind it down the shank in close turns to the tail, then back to the bead, to form a tapered body.

4 Secure the loose end of the wool behind the bead and remove the excess. Wind the copper wire over the wool body in open, evenly spaced turns. Secure the end of the wire behind the bead. Cast off the tying thread with a whip finish and trim the tail to a short stub.

RELATED SUBJECTS: • Weighting flies p24 • Fixing beads p25

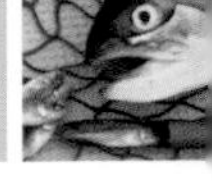

Hare's Ear Goldhead

trout on a Hare's Ear Goldhead.

Frank Sawyer's Killer Bug is both simple and deadly. Comprising a body made of beige wool wound over a lead-wire underbody, and bound together with turns of copper wire, it is difficult to think of a fly that is much easier to tie. In its original form the maggot-shaped body of the Killer Bug is purely impressionistic but makes a fair representation of a shrimp or a sedge pupa.

This version employs both a gold bead at the head and a short tag of fluorescent orange floss to give this otherwise subtly hued pattern a bit of a lift. The result is a superb fly. The bead used for the head may be gold, silver or even copper and it is worth keeping a few of each in the box. Changing colour is important because, in clear water, grayling can be put off by repeated drifts of the same fly through a shoal. The body colour originally came from the now-famous Chadwick's 477, a fine pinkish-beige darning wool that has since been discontinued. However, a number of materials suppliers stock a reasonable substitute.

Mike Weaver with a fine trout caught on the River Manulla, Co, Mayo, Ireland.

tip

- The Bead Sawyer Bug is an effective fly on all types of rivers and streams. Normally fished singly on a floating line, it is cast upstream and allowed to dead-drift with the current. In clear water it can be used to target individual fish by casting upstream far enough for the fly to sink to the same depth as the trout or grayling. When the fly drifts close to the target, a gentle lift of the rod causes the fly to rise – a motion that will often trigger a take.

Weighty Considerations

The weight of a fly is crucial in determining where it can be fished

Many patterns must be weighted with turns of wire or beads. Both wire and beads are difficult to secure and, without glue or many turns of thread, can slide up the shank.

The problem can be solved with an electric soldering iron. The solder fuses the wire to the hook shank and adds weight. It is simpler and subtler than adding metal beads because you can add as little or as much weight as you like – crucial when you want precise control over sink rate.

If necessary, you can add weight to quite small flies too, size 14 and smaller, without blocking the hook gape.

You can also position the weight at any point along the shank and even produce a bulging thorax.

Single layer of wire with solder on a size 14 hook: (left) humped and (below) slim

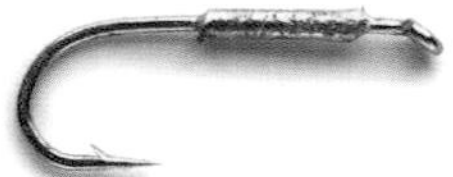

tip

• A nymph is more likely to be taken if it lingers in the trout's chosen feeding level for as long as possible. The closer to the surface the trout is feeding, the lighter the nymph should be. Conversely, if the trout are feeding hard on the bottom, a heavier version of the same nymph will sink to their level much more quickly and is less likely to be drawn upwards and away from the feeding trout on the retrieve. Dressing the fly on a lighter hook and adding a turn or two of soft hackle will also slow down the nymph's descent.

ADDING WEIGHT

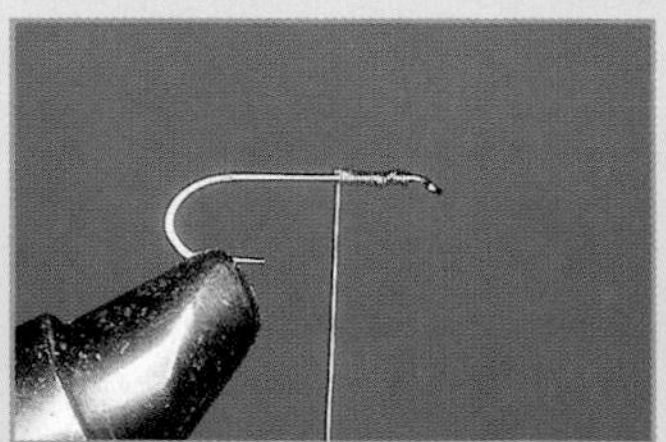

1 Wind one or two layers of copper or brass wire over the shank at the thorax area or wherever you want the weight.

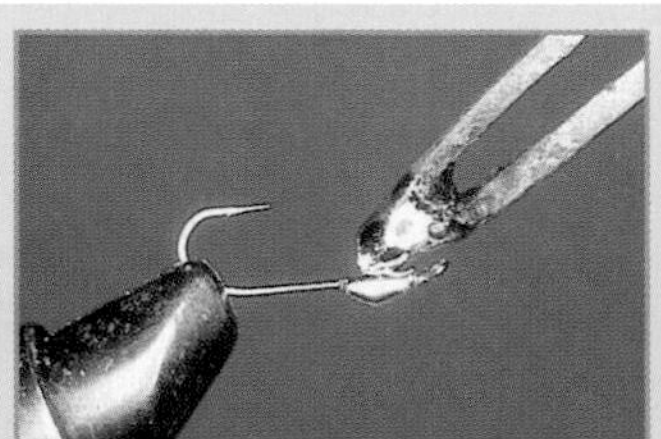

2 Apply a small amount of self-cleaning flux to the wire turns.

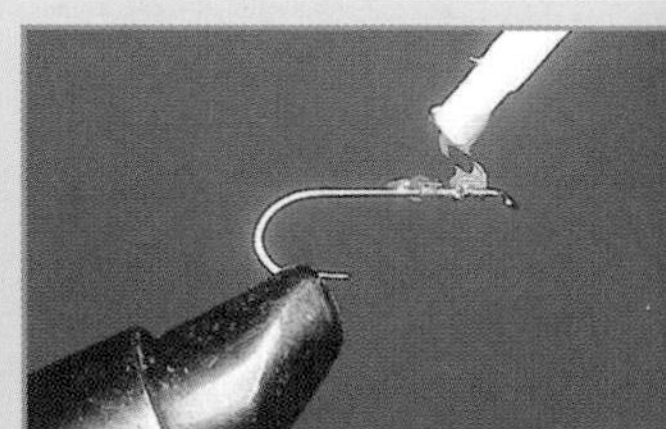

3 Heat up the electric soldering iron and apply molten solder to the wired thorax. Turning the hook upside down and using more solder to form a small blob underneath the hook produces a humped thorax.

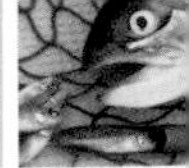

rattle and slide?

Do your gold beads rattle from side to side or slip down the hook shank? This will solve the problem while ribbing the fly at the same time.

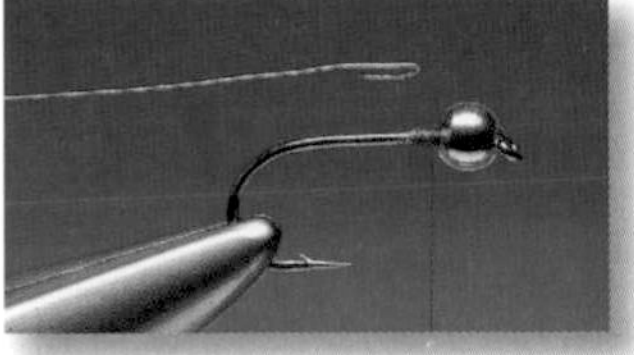

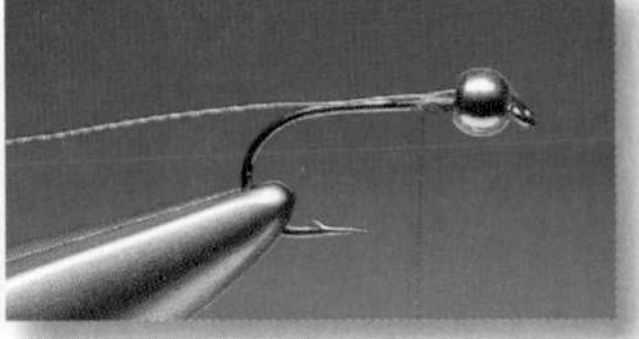

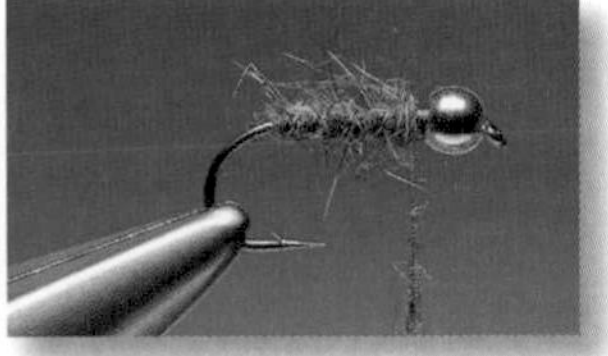

1 Slip the gold bead up to the eye. Run on the tying thread and build a base to accommodate the bead. Take a length of gold wire and, with tweezers, turn over one end to form a small loop.

2 Hold the wire and gently push the small loop into the recess at the rear of the bead. Secure the wire in place with tight thread wraps. This will hold the gold bead securely in place.

3 Complete the body of the fly then rib with the gold wire. Secure behind the bead with a whip finish.

tips

- Avoid copper wire coated in lacquer (reclaimed from armature windings).
- Be careful not to let the flux run into the eye of the hook – so will the solder.
- Do a batch of hooks at the same time and clean off the flux when cool.

Bug Life

Man-made fibres and plastic have revolutionized some aspects of fly-tying but there is nothing to beat the hare, the partridge and the pheasant for simulating essential 'buggyness' underwater

The Endrick Spider

Latex sheets, plastic legs and eyes can create perfect imitations of upwing nymphs and other creatures that inhabit the trout's larder. What they cannot do is give these creations life. Time and again fishermen have found that a general impression of 'buggyness', something that moves and twists in the current, that has subtle variations in tone and shading, will always out-fish a perfect, rigid replica of a particular creature.

For this elusive ingredient of buggyness, fly-fishermen have always looked to the sportsman's bag for natural materials in subtle variegation of browns, fawn and black.

The fur on a hare's ear (and elsewhere on its face and body) has an incredible variety of shades and textures from long dark guard hairs to soft, pale underfur, with every variation between. It is impossible to tie a fly with hare's ear fur that will not take fish.

Fibres from the long tail feathers of the common pheasant make a body of tiny, buggy, hairs. The male gives a rich chestnut red, the female a mottled grey-brown.

Partridge hackles, too, come in subtle shades of grey or brown, but each soft, mobile fibre is speckled with tiny dark bars that accentuate the smallest movement. A man could fish all his life with flies from these three materials and catch as much as any fisherman is entitled to.

MARCH BROWN
HOOK: Size 12–14 wet-fly
THREAD: Brown
TAIL: Brown partridge hackle
RIB: Fine gold wire
BODY: Dark hare's fur
WING: Hen pheasant secondary feathers
HACKLE: Brown partridge

March Brown

One of the buggyest flies ever created uses all three. The March Brown fly consistently takes trout in rivers where no natural march brown nymphs have ever swum.

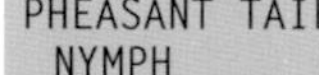

PHEASANT TAIL NYMPH
HOOK: Size 12–18
THREAD: Brown
TAIL: Cock pheasant tail fibres
RIB: Copper wire
BODY: Cock pheasant tail
THORAX: Cock pheasant tail

Pheasant Tail Nymph

The Pheasant Tail Nymph needs no introduction. It is simply the first and best nymph to try if trout are taking ephemerid (upwing) nymphs beneath the surface.

RELATED SUBJECT: • Weighting flies p24

Endrick Spider

The Endrick Spider has features of both these famous flies. It is perfectly designed for fishing in fast-flowing water. Its slim, heavily weighted body allows it to sink quickly so that it keeps well below the surface even when allowed to swing across the current.

It was initially tied by John Harwood to catch salmon and sea trout, but has turned out to be a great fly for brown trout and grayling. With its hackle of brown partridge, the Endrick Spider makes an effective representation of any number of aquatic life-forms, from a shrimp to the nymphs of various medium-sized, dark upwings. The ability to simply represent something alive and edible is where this fly excels.

tip

- The Endrick Spider works best when fished down-and-across, in the standard wet-fly technique for rivers. It may be fished singly, on a floating line, but is often used as part of a team where, because it is heavy, it is used as the point fly. It will catch fish wherever trout or grayling are feeding subsurface.

ENDRICK SPIDER

HOOK: **Size 8–12**

THREAD: **Black or brown**

UNDERBODY: **Copper or fine lead wire**

TAIL: **Cock pheasant tail fibres**

RIB: **Fine gold wire**

BODY: **Cock pheasant tail fibres**

HACKLE: **Brown partridge hackle**

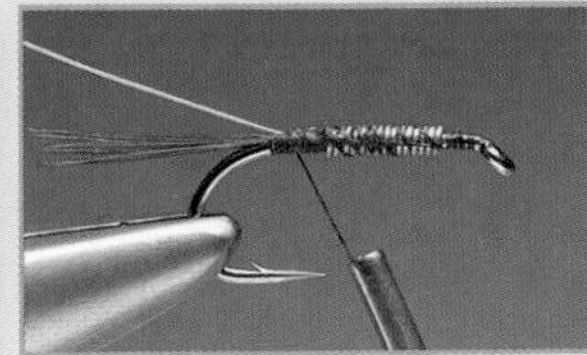

1 Wind on an underbody of close turns of the fine lead or copper wire. Secure with tying thread. Carry the thread down to the bend. Catch in a few fibres of cock pheasant tail (PT) plus 2in of fine gold wire.

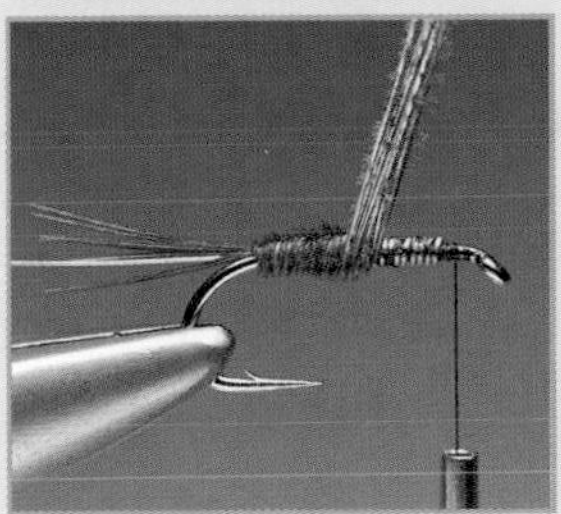

2 Take a second bunch of cock pheasant tail fibres. Catch them in by their tips at the base of the tail. Carry the thread up the shank, stopping a short distance from the eye. Allowing the fibres of pheasant tail to spread flat, wind them over the underbody until they reach the thread. Secure with the thread.

3 Wind the wire rib over the pheasant tail in the opposite spiral. This ensures that the wire locks the PT in place. Secure and trim rib. Select a small, well-marked brown partridge hackle. Stroke the feather fibres away from the tip. Trim the tip to a short stub and catch it in just in front of the body.

4 Wind on two full turns. Stroke the hackle fibres back down the body and secure the stem of the hackle at the eye.

Mr Stewart's Special Spiders

Spider patterns are some of the oldest and simplest of flies, widely used because they still work wonderfully well

Slim but deadly: Stewart's Black Spider and Dun and Orange Spider

tying stewart spiders

- To give of their best, Spiders must be tied on fine-wire hooks.
- Soft hackles with fine fibres still provide plenty of mass, yet allow the fly to retain that all-important translucency. The starling hackle used on Stewart's Black Spider is as perfect a hackle feather as you can find. Would that they came in colours other than black. Game-bird hackles are recommended when tying palmered Spiders, but some, such as those from coots and pheasants, are best avoided as they are too dense to produce a delicate and lively fly. Hackles from domestic capes are acceptable and it is no bad thing to rummage around in the bargain bin of a tackle shop. Very often a few pennies will buy you a cape of an indescribable but most useful shade.

STEWART'S BLACK SPIDER

This is the fly that started it all and an undisputed classic. Use three of them on the same leader with confidence.

HOOK: **Size 14–18**

BODY: **Waxed dark brown thread**

HACKLE: **Black glossy feather from a cock starling. A natural black hen hackle can substitute for starling.**

DUN AND ORANGE

This favourite comes into its own during spinner falls. when fish gorge on spent upwinged flies.

HOOK: **Size 14–18**

BODY: **Waxed orange thread**

HACKLE: **Light dun hen hackle or starling underwing.**

WC Stewart revealed these special Spiders in *The Practical Angler* (1857). Like most Spiders, they were fashioned from tying silks and soft hackles plucked from wild birds, but the hackle was wound through the first third of the fly's body to give a semi-translucent fly with bags of bounce: in short, exactly what is needed to imitate a struggling insect, a trigger that trout can seldom resist.

What gives the Stewart-style Spiders their edge? Apart from the usual Spider traits of slimness and translucence, their palmered hackles give them an uncannily natural look possessed by few other flies employed to imitate emerging flies, drowned and stillborn duns. There's no doubt that the palmered hackle mimics wonderfully well a sedge pupa with its shuck full of gas rising to the surface to hatch; and when it comes to small, dark terrestrials, it's difficult to find anything to beat Stewart's original Black Spider.

Stewart Spiders can be deadly during those frustrating spinner falls when trout target flies drifting in the surface film. It is difficult enough to follow low-riding spinner imitations in daylight – at dusk it's impossible. Have faith in a team of three Spiders, two feet apart. Pitch them slightly up and across the stream, keep the rod-point high throughout the retrieve to allow fish sufficient slack line to turn down with the fly without feeling any resistance. Where the current slackens, cast more squarely across the flow and make an upstream mend to let the Spiders sink a little before allowing them to ride naturally downstream, tracking their progress with the rod tip.

While a take may occur at any time, pay special attention when the Spiders begin to accelerate across the current and when they come to rest directly below you. Keep your eyes on the tip of the fly-line: as it draws confidently away, lift the rod and you're in business.

A Bit Below the Surface

An ingenious solution to the problem of finicky feeders

Some of the most successful and innovative developments in fly dressing do not affect how the fly appears to the trout: they affect where the fly appears. Czech Nymphs reached, for the first time, fish that did not want to budge from the bottom of fast rivers. There are times, especially on hard-fished rivers, when trout and grayling will refuse dry flies and conventional nymphs but will take a fly drifting just beneath the surface. They want the fly in the top inch of the water or not at all.

The Parasol Nymph is a clever little pattern designed to exploit the trout's liking for a fly drifting just under the surface. This ingenious style of tying was made popular in America by Jim Schollmeyer and Ted Leeson for waters where the trout had become wary of more conventional presentations. Wide, slow pools on bright days often demand long casts that are inevitably ruined by drag. A midge pupa dressed Parasol style will often solve the problem. A tiny degree of micro-drag, imperceptible to the fisherman, can ruin the chances of a dry-fly on the surface

Parasol caddis pupa in action

the parasol technique

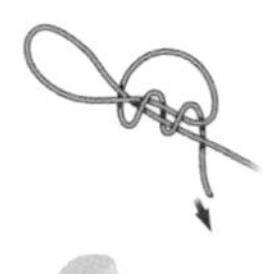

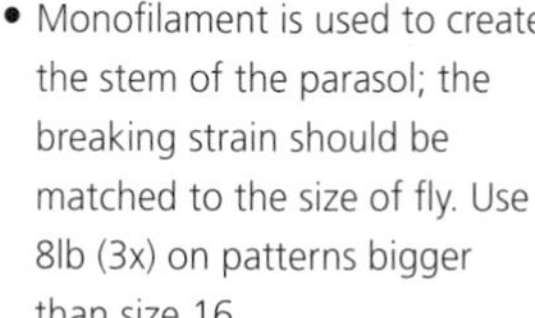

- Monofilament is used to create the stem of the parasol; the breaking strain should be matched to the size of fly. Use 8lb (3x) on patterns bigger than size 16.

- A single Grinner knot creates a running noose that can be eased down on the yarn, which is then permanently fixed with a blob of varnish. If you have problems fixing the nylon stem to the hook, crimp the end with pliers.

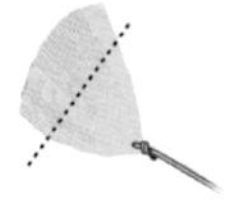

- The poly yarn fluffs out nicely into a uniform parasol if the tuft is teased out with a dubbing needle or a fine comb. A ¼in tuft is adequate on size 12–14 hooks. The denser the tuft, the more buoyant it will be.
- While white yarn is a good all-round colour, when the light is really poor, a brighter yarn stands out well. Incorporating two contrasting colours of yarn in the parasol is the answer to fishing in dappled light: as the fly drifts in and out of the different intensities of light, one of the two colours will be highly visible.
- The length of the nylon stem governs at what depth the nymph will be suspended. To avoid the fly 'helicoptering' and creating tangles, use a stem of around ½in or less.

RELATED SUBJECT:
- High-visibilty wings p36

of a slow pool, but trout are much more tolerant of (or find it harder to detect) the same degree of drag just below the surface. It may even enhance the fly by imparting a little 'life' to the artificial. The tuft supporting the parasol nymph may be dragging slightly in the surface but that doesn't seem to trouble the trout.

The Parasol style of tying has tremendous potential and can be applied to a whole range of flies. Imitations of terrestrial insects and spent flies which drown and drift along just beneath the surface film are obvious candidates for the parasol treatment, along with tried and tested favourites like the Pheasant Tail Nymph and Hare's Ear. This style of tying is not the answer to all our prayers but Parasol-style flies can get you out of jail with some demanding fish, and even if called upon only once or twice a season.

PARASOL CADDIS PUPA

This one is ideal for those frantic sedge hatches on long summer evenings. Keep the abdomen dubbing compact so that the pupa penetrates the surface film on touchdown. A slightly bigger bright yellow tuft stands out in the failing light.

HOOK: Size 14 grub

THREAD: Tan

RIB: Brown Flexifloss

ABDOMEN: Cream dubbing

PARASOL: Clear nylon and yellow poly yarn

THORAX: Natural hare or grey squirrel

LEGS: Partridge hackle fibres

PARASOL BRASSIE

Brassies are a favourite fly and can be devastating when presented a fraction beneath the film. Other useful colours include an all-black version and one tied using a wine-coloured wire.

HOOK: Size 18-22

THREAD: Orange

BODY: Bright orange Wapsi Ultra

PARASOL: Orange poly yarn

THORAX: Natural mole's fur

PARASOL MIDGE

HOOK: Size 20-24 TMC 2487

THREAD: Black 14/0 Sheer

RIB: Fine silver wire

ABDOMEN: Black tying thread

PARASOL: Clear nylon and soft pink poly yarn

WING BUDS: Single strand fluorescent orange thread

THORAX: Black Superfine dubbing

TWO-TONE PARASOL PTN

The two-tone yarn is highly visible under most light variables, especially when targeting tree-lined runs where the fly drifts in and out of shadows.

HOOK: Size 12–16

THREAD: Tan

RIB: Fine copper wire

TAIL AND BODY: Cock pheasant tail fibres

PARASOL: Black and white poly yarn

THORAX: Rabbit or squirrel fur

Accident and Emergency - the Sedge

Trout have a weakness for insects at their most vulnerable.

The most hazardous moments in the life of caddis or upwinged fly are the seconds spent hatching at the water's surface. The creature must break out of the pupal or nymphal skin, break through the cloying skin of the water's surface tension and scramble aloft to ride the current while the wings unfold and inflate before lift off. This takes time and a glitch at any stage can trap the struggling creature in the clinging grip of surface tension. Accidents are common and usually prove fatal. Even if everything goes well, the emerging insect is helpless for a few moments which may be all an approaching trout needs.

Traditional dry-flies ride the surface on a cushion of hackle tips, imitating the legs of the adult held above the surface. To imitate the insect at the vulnerable point of hatching, the fly must lie awash in the water surface itself.

Several modern patterns exploit the waterlogged look in order to entice the trout.

tips

- The Balloon Caddis works on any river where sedges abound. It is most effective when the fish are taking the naturals close to or in the water's surface. Major hatches of these medium-sized sedges take place throughout the summer, particularly on warm evenings.
- Fished singly on a floating line and a tapered leader, the pattern is cast upstream and allowed to dead-drift in a lively current. It can work well if given an occasional twitch to mimic the movement of the natural.

Choosing the fly for the hatch

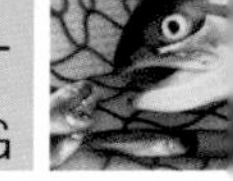

The Balloon Caddis

Austrian fly-fisher Roman Moser developed an innovative pattern to imitate a sedge (caddis) fly emerging from its pupal skin right at the water's surface. In order to get the profile as realistic as possible, it uses buoyant, closed-cell foam rather than a hackle to keep it afloat.

The yellow foam thorax not only helps to keep the fly floating, it provides a distinct hump, very like that created by the emerging adult sedge. Because of this, the Balloon Caddis is a deadly pattern when both trout and grayling are taking sedges in that half-in, half-out stage. Additional buoyancy comes from a wing of deer or elk hair, dyed brown in the original version, tied low over a body of dubbed fur. The body itself is tied quite full to represent the plump body of the sedge pupa and may be tied in either amber or green.

When using foam it is important not to overstretch it, as this compresses the tiny bubbles and reduces its buoyancy. Unlike when using a thin plastic strip, the foam is merely folded over and secured in position with tying thread. Also, don't skimp on the amount of foam used as this, too, will prevent the finished fly from floating properly.

BALLOON CADDIS

HOOK: Size 10–14 wet-fly

THREAD: Yellow

BODY: Green or amber Antron

WING: Deer or elk hair

THORAX: Yellow micro-cellular foam

TYING THE BALLOON CADDIS

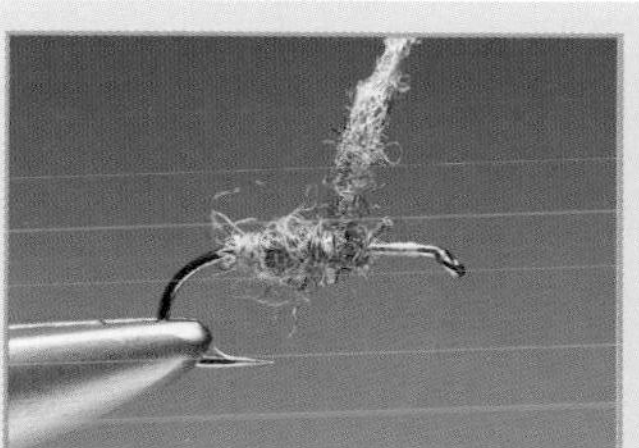

1 Run the tying thread down the shank to the bend. Take a large pinch of green Antron. Dub it on to the thread to form a coarse rope and then wind along the shank in close turns to create a chunky abdomen two-thirds of the way to the eye.

2 Take a bunch of dyed-brown deer hair. Remove any damaged fibres and place the tips roughly level. Now position the wing with two or three turns of thread.

3 Secure the wing with further tight turns of thread, trim hair stubs and cover the waste ends with more tight turns of thread.

4 Catch in a strip of yellow microcellular foam approximately ¼in wide. The waste end should fill the gap between the eye and the wing base.

5 Wind the thread to the wing base then fold the foam over to meet it. Don't pull the foam tight, as this will reduce its buoyancy. Secure with turns of thread and a whip finish. Trim the foam so that the trailing end sits just over the wing base. Finally, run a small amount of clear varnish into the thread wraps to secure the foam strip in place.

Accident and Emergency – the Upwing Dun

One of the most frustrating times in a fisherman's life comes when he finds himself surrounded by drifting duns. Trout are rising right and left, taking something from the surface but ignoring the angler's beautifully tied imitation of the dun. Trout like an easy life. They will often concentrate their efforts on those insects still struggling to hatch through the surface and in no imminent danger of taking off. It's easier that way.

The Sparkle Dun

The Sparkle Dun lies in the surface film, still attached to its nymphal shuck. This fly is a modification of the original Comparadun developed by American anglers Al Caucci and Bob Nastasi more than 20 years ago. The interesting feature of this pattern is the combined wing and hackle, which is made of deer-hair tips tied to form a semi-circle around the top

SPARKLE DUN

HOOK: Size 12–16 down-eyed dry-fly

THREAD: Olive

TAIL: Clear Antron yarn

BODY: Fine, olive synthetic dubbing

WING: Deer-hair tips

HEAD: Fine, olive synthetic dubbing

TYING THE SPARKLE DUN

1 Wind a solid base for the wing. Take a generous pinch of plain deer hair with nicely mottled tips. Remove any fluff and broken hairs and make sure the tips are even. Catch the bunch in with loose thread turns so that it projects well past the eye.

2 Secure the bunch with further tight thread turns, allowing the hair to flare around the top and sides but not underneath the hook. Trim away the waste, staggering the cuts, then cover with turns of thread to form a tapered body.

3 Carry the thread down to the bend. Tie in a few strands of clear Antron yarn to suggest the nymphal shuck of the hatching dun. Dub on the body material and form the body by winding the dubbed thread in touching turns.

4 Bend the wing back, letting it flare into a semicircle. Fix in place with turns of thread in front of the wing. Dub on more material and wind the front section of body tight against the wing to support it in the semicircular shape. Whip finish.

RELATED SUBJECT:

• Controlling deer hair p65

and sides of the hook. This allows the dubbing abdomen of the fly to lie in the surface. The fly is extremely durable because the deer hair is far tougher than delicate feather fibres.

The pattern may be tied in a wide range of sizes and body colours to imitate anything from the largest mayfly to the tiniest pale watery dun. However, it is as an imitation of a small- to medium-sized olive that the pattern has become so well-known.

In the original Comparadun, the tail consisted of the same deer-hair tips used for the wing. In the Sparkle Dun, a few strands of clear Antron are used in the tail to suggest the nymphal shuck from which the dun has just emerged. You can buy purpose-made Irise Shuck Tails (Lureflash) to re-create these empty shucks.

Stalking on a chalkstream

tip

- This Sparkle Dun is an effective fly for any river or stream, but especially those with a good hatch of small- to medium-sized olives. It will work both in broken water and glides and is a great all-round imitation of a number of upwinged duns.

flush with success

- If a trout refuses your dry-fly even when it is a good imitation of what's hatching, trim the hackle underneath so the fly sits flush with the surface. Trout will often refuse a high-riding fly but will take one awash in the surface film.

King Klink

How the Klinkhamer Special conquered the world

The Klinkhamer was invented by Hans van Klinken and was initially called the LT (Light Tan) Caddis because of the colour of its abdomen. The original tying superbly echoed many caddis and their pupae. But Klinkhamers also made their mark when fished as a general search pattern, especially in faster water.

John Roberts included the fly in his book *The World's Best Trout Flies*, and Partridge of Redditch made a hook (the GRS15ST) for the sole purpose of accommodating the dressing.

The large and highly visible wing ensures that you are always aware of the Klinkhamer's whereabouts. The slightly oversized hackle provides stability and, with the abdomen hanging subsurface, fish have more than enough to latch on to.

But what of the Klinkhamer's credentials as an all-rounder? Take caenis, a bugbear for many flyfishers, their diminutive size and overwhelming presence often intimidating the most seasoned of anglers. Tie the tiny wing post with bright orange or pink yarn and it is conspicuous in the maelstrom of hatching duns. As for the upwinged flies, a Klinkhamer that corresponds

KLINKHAMER SPECIAL

HOOK: Partridge GRS15ST, size 8–18

THREAD: Grey or tan

BODY: Fine dubbing in suitable colour

THORAX: Peacock herl

HACKLE: Cock hackle to suit body colour

WING: White poly yarn

TYING THE KLINKHAMER SPECIAL

1 Tie on the thread behind the hook eye winding it down the shank and back to a point one-third of the shank length from the eye. Position the winging material on top of the hook and bind down.

2 Cut a taper on the yarn, covering the waste end with turns of thread before finishing at the bend. On smaller flies, attach the yarn bow-tie fashion on top of the hook shank.

3 Having taken the thread some way back up the shank, apply a noodle of dubbing to the thread. With touching turns, form a neat, tapered abdomen, finishing a fraction behind the wing.

4 Catch in an appropriate hackle with a little exposed stem and take the thread 4–5 turns high, up the wing, providing a secure post for the hackle and trapping the bare stem at the same time.

RELATED SUBJECT: • New Zealand style droppers p50 and 53

to the natural's overall appearance excels during the early part of a hatch when fish are nailing nymphs on the point of hatching. Even when trout are busy on the fully emerged duns, they will have an eye for a carefully presented Klinkhamer pattern. And with the spinner fall, a mahogany-coloured fly with a pale dun hackle has its moments, too. A mayfly pattern based on the Klinkhamer is invaluable during the early days of this ephemerid carnival when timid trout can easily be overwhelmed by the sheer size of naturals. Acting like an iceberg, with its bulk submerged, a Klinkhamer is readily taken. Remember to increase leader diameter to prevent a twisting tippet.

The Klinkhamer lends itself to the New Zealand dropper method – a nymph tied to a short length of monofilament and attached to the hook bend. On those rare occasions when fish refuse to come the extra yard for a dry-fly, a trailing nymph can play its part.

Acting as emerger, dun, drowned fly and virtually anything else that fish care to eat, the Klinkhamer is one of the most versatile patterns ever.

tips on tying

- Use very fine material for the body, which should instantly penetrate the surface film to ensure the Klinkhamer sits correctly. Use thread for flies smaller than size 20.
- The iridescence of peacock herl creates a stunning thorax which adds to the fly's attraction. Its shortcoming is fragility so twist the three strands of herl round the tying thread.
- For wing colour, apart from obvious white, shades like orange, yellow, pink – even black – have their place. Try a two-tone wing for changing light conditions.
- Hans suggests hackle colours of blue dun, light ginger and chestnut brown. Grizzle works well on terrestrial patterns. Even on black flies, steer clear of a black hackle: it is too dense when viewed from below.

5 Wind down the post and attach three strands of peacock herl. Apply varnish to the thread post for strength and around the thorax to help bind the herl. Twist the herl around the thread.

6 Working either side of the wing, wind a dense thorax region, being careful not to trap any hackle fibres. On the final turn of the thorax make sure it comes to rest around the post base.

7 Starting from the top of the post, carefully wind the hackle so each turn sits under the previous turn. Work the hackle downwards, towards the thorax.

8 Having applied 4–5 turns, secure the hackle with thread, working around the wing base. Snip away surplus hackle and complete with a 4-turn whip finish. Cut the wing to length.

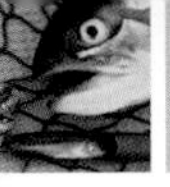

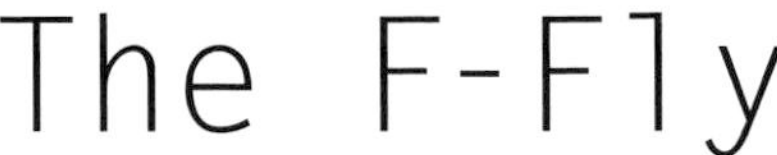

The F-Fly

As easy to tie as a shoelace, the F-Fly is one of the deadliest dry-flies ever invented

Dry-flies that rely on cul-de-canard (CDC), the frond-like plumes plucked from around a duck's preen gland, for their incredible buoyancy have been used by Swiss anglers for many years but it is to Slovenia's Marjan Fratnik that fly-fishers the world over owe a vote of thanks. In 1983, inspired by a fly sent him by innovative Swiss fly-fisher Jules Rindlisbacher, Marjan developed his own much simplified version for fishing the ice-cold alpine rivers and chalk streams that provide some of the finest brown trout and grayling fishing to be found anywhere in the world.

The original F-Fly had no body or hackle and was nothing more than a pinch of fibres plucked from a CDC plume and bound to a hook. Those tied on hooks smaller than a size 18 used only a single plume, those up to a size 14 had two: anything bigger used three plumes.

Marjan added a very sparsely dubbed grey body and later versions have bodies formed from hare's ear and fine dubbings of every kind and colour, but whether they are any more successful than the original bare hook – which penetrated the surface instantly – is doubtful.

F-FLY

HOOK: Size 10–20
THREAD: To match body colour
BODY: Fine dubbings in grey, black, olive, brown, tan and hare's ear
WING: Natural CDC fibres

tips

- Match the size to the hatching insect, be it of olives, sedges or in a fall of terrestrials of any colour, and the F-Fly can be used with complete confidence. A size 14 version with a pale olive body and a light wing is especially good. Trout feeding on black gnats, hawthorns and all manner of terrestrials will respond to an F-Fly with a dark brown or black body.
- Fish it singly. On a stillwater, the F-Fly should be cast into the path of a moving fish and left to its own devices. On a river allow it to drift without any vestige of drag.

TYING THE F-FLY

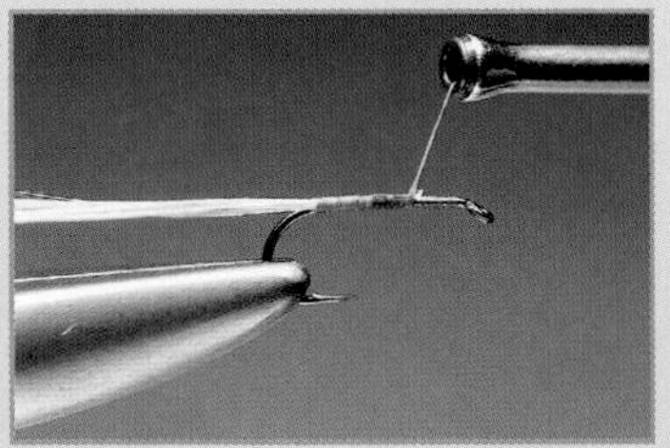

1 Run the thread in touching turns to a point just opposite the barb. Secure in the ribbing tinsel and the slim bunch of herls to form the body.

2 Wind the body with touching turns of the herls. Wind the rib in evenly spaced turns. Trim off waste rib and herls.

3 Offer up the natural brown CDC plumes with the tips extending just past the bend. Tie in the CDC fibres on top of the hook. If the wing is too long, nip off the ends with your fingernails. Trim the stub and form a neat head. That's all there is to it.

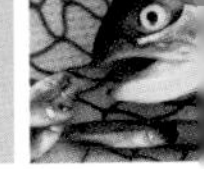

the myth and magic

'I cannot remember who told me that the feathers from the duck's arse owed their floating properties to the oil from the bird's preen gland, and that once the oil was gone, the fly was no good. I certainly believed it, and I certainly passed it on; so I can be said to have contributed to its acceptance as piscatorial gospel.

'I am now informed by my friend, Marjan Fratnik – the inventor of the incomparable F-Fly and the man who, more than any other, put CDC on the map – that this is all nonsense.

'According to Fratnik, the fly floats because of the structure of the feather, and stops floating when the structure collapses as a result of the fly becoming saturated or coated in fish slime. Thorough drying (Fratnik used a hair-dryer) restores the floating properties entirely, and the presence or absence of preen gland oil has nothing to do with it.' TOM FORT

Little Black Number

Terrestrial insects were never designed for the water and make easy pickings

Many land-based insects meet a watery end, either falling or being blown on to the surface at any time of the day, and imitations are most likely to be successful precisely when there are no aquatic hatches commanding the trout's attention.

There are times when terrestrial flies are a fish's principal food source and will be selected in preference to aquatic flies. One 12in trout was found to have nearly 200 hawthorn flies in its stomach. In the stomach of another, 1,800 black gnats have been found.

Terrestrial flies are most important on small streams with overhanging foliage but they can be found on any water, particularly on windy days as the season progresses. Dr Woolland's survey on the River Dee examined the stomach contents of 105 brown trout over a year. Two-thirds of the contents were winged insects – that is, adults rather than larvae or pupae. Of these, over half the total were terrestrial insects such as beetles, various bugs, hawthorn flies, black gnats, and crane-flies.

Terrestrial insects can turn up on any water. Crane-fly imitations (daddy-long-legs, often called daddys) and beetles are covered in the section on stillwaters. Every river fisherman should always carry a selection of little black numbers to imitate the hawthorn flies of spring and the black gnats of summer.

tip

- If the trout begin to nudge rather than take the high-floating dry-fly, trim all the cock hackle fibres from beneath the body or fish it untreated so that it sits in or just below the surface.

TYING THE HAWTHORN FLY

1 Catch in a length of black Flexifloss. Bind down the Flexifloss just round the bend. Dub on the black seal's fur to form a slender body.

2 Stop well short of the hook eye; remove any excess dubbing. Rib the body, keeping the Flexifloss under steady tension.

3 Knot two dyed pheasant tail fibres to represent a knee. Repeat and tie in the knotted legs, one on each side of the thorax. Hold the Antron wing in place on top of the body and secure it in with several tight turns of thread.

4 Catch in a black cock hackle. Dub on a little more black seal's fur and form the thorax, then wind the hackle through the thorax in open turns. Trim and make a small head with a whip finish.

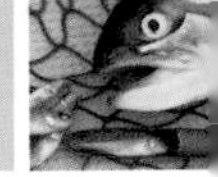

Hawthorn Fly

This large, hairy-bodied, gangly-legged insect provides an early-season treat for trout and grayling. They can appear in huge numbers, usually in late April, and last for 2–3 weeks. The dressing for the Black Gnat is very similar but usually tied on a smaller hook to match the smaller natural gnats of the summer. For such smaller flies, omit the legs but tease out the black dubbing of the body to give the fly its characteristic 'buzz'.

> HAWTHORN FLY
>
> HOOK: Size 10–12
>
> THREAD: Black
>
> BODY: Black seal's fur, black Antron
>
> RIB: Black Flexifloss
>
> LEGS: Knotted black pheasant tail fibres
>
> WINGS: White Antron or white CDC or mottled grey Wonderwing
>
> HACKLE: Black cock

A fall of hawthorn flies can mean a bonanza for the angler with the right artificial

Griffiths Gnat

Sometimes the fish of summer become preoccupied with tiny black flies and refuse anything bigger. Try offering them a Griffiths Gnat, which is easier to tie in sizes down to 24 and has plenty of buzz.

> GRIFFITHS GNAT
>
> HOOK: Size 16–24 down-eyed dry-fly
>
> THREAD: Black
>
> TAIL *(optional)*: Orange or lime-green fluorescent yarn or Pearl Twinkle
>
> BODY: Peacock herl
>
> HACKLE: Short-fibred grizzle cock hackle

Dry-fly Tradition

This quartet of dry-flies has been taking trout for longer than any of us have been fishing. The youngest, the Adams, was first tied in 1922. They are all very good general-purpose flies but they excel in hatches of the dry-fly fisherman's favourite flies, the various species of upwinged flies he refers to as 'the olives'

Greenwell's Glory

This is among the most famous of all British trout flies. The pattern was first tied as a wet-fly on the River Tweed in the mid-nineteenth century. One hundred and fifty years later it still makes a very good imitation of all the olive upwings.

Some modern commercial versions use olive floss for the body but the secret of the fly's phenomenal success lies in the thorough waxing of the yellow silk. This creates the olive hue: it also makes the thread translucent – an effect that can't be replicated by the opaque floss. This dry-fly version of the Greenwell's can be tied with or without a tail.

GREENWELL'S GLORY

- HOOK: Size 14–16 dry-fly
- THREAD: Yellow or primrose silk
- TAIL *(optional)*: Furnace cock hackle
- BODY: Well-waxed yellow or primrose tying silk
- RIB: Fine gold wire
- HACKLE: Furnace cock hackle
- WING: Starling or mallard primary

Adams

This American original is probably the most popular and widely used dry-fly in the UK. It is a superb general representation of a whole range of upwinged flies and so can be used with confidence on any water with natural olives. While the combination of grey and brown might not seem ideal for imitating flies that are mostly various shades of olive, the Adams still manages to tempt fish whether they are feeding on a miscellany of food or whether they are targeting a specific hatch. The blend of grizzle and brown cock hackle fibres is particularly effective: the Adams is a very lively looking fly.

The Adams is tied in a range of forms, from the standard one with hackle-point wings and a collar hackle to parachute and thorax-tied versions. Because of its versatility it is tied in a huge range of sizes. A size 8 makes a good representation of a mayfly while, on a size 22, it can cover even the smallest caenis.

ADAMS

- HOOK: Size 8–22 medium to lightweight dry-fly
- THREAD: Black or brown
- TAIL: Grizzle and brown cock hackle fibres
- BODY: Grey rabbit or muskrat underfur
- HACKLE: Grizzle and brown cock hackles
- WING: Grizzle hackle points

RELATED SUBJECT: • Teasing out dubbing p87

GREY DUSTER
HOOK: Size 10–16
THREAD: Grey
TAIL *(optional)*: Badger cock hackle fibres
BODY: A blend of blueish-grey rabbit underfur and guard hairs
HACKLE: Well-marked badger cock

Grey Duster

Another superb all-purpose dry-fly, used to imitate a whole host of insects. On tiny hooks it is a useful caenis imitation; a little bigger and it works well when stone-flies and various olive duns are being taken. Dressed on a size 10 hook with a bushier than normal hackle, it will fool trout feeding on mayflies when more elaborately dressed imitations are scorned.

Many insects are quite light in colour on hatching, which probably accounts for the trout's willingness to accept the Grey Duster as a new adult. The strong contrast between the black centre and pale cream fringe of the badger hackle makes it easy to see: the Grey Duster is a favourite pattern for fishing at dusk.

think backward

- When fishing heavily bushed streams, fly losses can be kept to a minimum by reversing the dressing so that the hackles mask the hook and help the fly bounce off the vegetation.

GOLD-RIBBED HARE'S EAR
HOOK: Size 14–18 dry-fly
THREAD: Brown or yellow
TAIL: A few hare's body hairs
BODY: Dark hare's fur
RIB: Flat gold tinsel
HACKLE: Teased-out fibres of hare's fur
WING: Paired slips of starling or mallard primary

Gold-ribbed Hare's Ear

One of the most effective of all artificial flies, this dry fly is sometimes tied with blue dun cock hackle but it is more effective in the smaller sizes tied without a hackle, relying on the teased-out fibres of the hare's ear to keep it afloat. Tied this way, the fly sits low on the water, the hair simulating the struggles of a hatching dun. In larger sizes, especially if the fly is to be fished in fast-flowing water, it is worth adding a cock hackle to prevent the fly from sinking. The starling wing is optional but it does make the low-riding hackle-less fly easier to see.

steaming idea

- Flies with crumpled tails and wings can be given a new lease of life if they are held in the steam from a kettle.

Backward Beauty

For the trout who has seen it all

The Devaux Dun is a deadly dry-fly whenever olives are on the water, especially the large dark olives of spring. It comes from The House of Devaux in Champagnole, a small town in the heart of the Jura mountains of north-eastern France, a region threaded with crystal limestone rivers.

The Devaux Dun uses a style of dressing originally devised by Neil Patterson in his famous Funneldun. The name describes the way the hackle surrounds the eye like a funnel. This ensures that the fly will sit the right way up with the hackle fibres dimpling the water, simulating a fly caught in the highly vulnerable act of breaking through the surface. At this critical stage the fly, a struggling tangle of legs and budding wings, is the easiest of pickings – but not for long. This rearranging of body parts takes just a few seconds, after which the fly will be as free as the air. The trout knows it, hence the savage rise to the Devaux Dun.

Like other patterns that have the hackle pointing out over the eye, the fibres on the hackle feather,

tip

- Although devised for river work, the Devaux Dun is also a deadly fly on stillwaters when olives are about.

TYING THE DEVAUX DUN

1 Remove the fluffy fibres from the base of the hackle feather and secure it on top of the hook shank with a few tight turns of thread.

2 Wind the hackle in touching turns.

3 Finish winding the hackle, tie it down and snip away the unwanted feather.

7 Tie in the ribbing thread on the far side of the hook and counter-spin the bobbin to take out any twists.

8 To achieve translucence, wax the tying thread. The same technique is used to create the body of the Greenwell's Glory (see page 42).

9 Form the body by winding the well-waxed thread over the butt end of the tail fibres. Start to rib the body with the thick black thread.

or feathers, should be half as long again as one usually chosen for a normal dry-fly of the same size. This also uses up those hackles that are too long for a standard dry-fly. While not difficult to tie, the Devaux Dun has an unusual tying sequence: the materials are laid on in reverse order. Because the hackles stretch forward over the eye, the Devaux Dun is best tied on a hook with a short shank and a wide gape.

If you lack the red game dyed-olive hackle used in this version of the Dun, then combine two hackles – one a red game, the other a brownish olive – to achieve the right colour. If you take this option, tie in the red game hackle first and wind on a couple of full turns and then tie it down. Snip away the waste feather and, working towards the bend, make all secure with five turns of thread before tying in the second hackle. Make three turns and secure it. Snip away the unwanted hackle feather and, from that point, carry on as if the hackle had been formed with the single feather.

DEVAUX DUN

HOOK: Size 14–18 with a wide gape

THREAD: Primrose silk

TAIL: Good bunch of rusty dun cock hackles

BODY: Well-waxed primrose silk

RIB: Black thread

HACKLE: A red game cock hackle dyed a brownish-olive and forced forwards by turns of tying thread

WINGS *(optional)*: Blue dun hen hackle points or CDC fibres

4 The winged version – a bunch of CDC plumes can also be used – calls for a matched pair of small blue dun hackles.

5 Tie in the hackle-point wings to slope well out over the hook eye.

6 Trim a bunch of rusty dun cock hackle fibres and tie them in on top of the hook shank.

10 Complete the ribbing and tie it down with several more turns of the waxed thread.

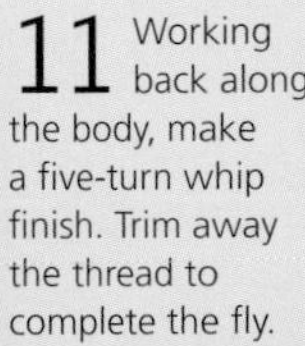

11 Working back along the body, make a five-turn whip finish. Trim away the thread to complete the fly.

Footprints on the Water

A super-realistic dun for educated trout

For centuries, anglers have been lashing fur and feather on to hooks in an attempt to imitate the insects on which trout feed. It is generally accepted that trout take an artificial floating fly because it presents a footprint or points of light similar to that made by the natural insect standing on the surface.

The Devaux Dun and Neil Patterson's Funneldun are deadly flies, yet, being somewhat outside the usual style of dry-fly design, they are rarely seen beyond the fly boxes of the most dedicated chalk stream prowlers. Likewise, the USD (UpSideDown) Paradun created by John Goddard and Brian Clarke is an excellent pattern to turn to when things get difficult, but it is time-consuming and tricky to build. These immensely effective flies create a footprint very similar to that of the natural insect at rest on the surface.

This ingenious pattern from Roy Christie has a simple design, uses familiar techniques and takes no great skill at the vice, but a couple of minor changes produce a fly to fool the most sophisticated fish.

It is called the Easy-Peasy USD Dun. It can be tied to imitate any of the upwinged flies: simply adapt your own favourite patterns, using the time-proven recipes, to this style of dressing.

How much dressing is added depends very much on where the fly is to be used. Dress them lightly for lakes and slow flows, more densely for turbulent streams, and very heavily hackled for dapping.

The big difference between this fly and a standard dry-fly is that it lands with the hook point skywards and with the body on or above the surface, so producing that all-important footprint or points of light on the surface.

TYING THE EASY-PEASY USD DUN

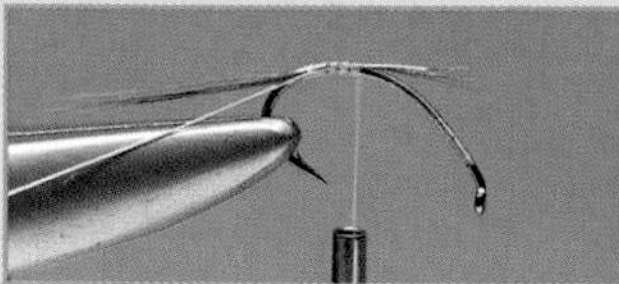

1 Run the tying thread from the eye to a point about a third of the way round the bend. Catch in the rib and the tail fibres to extend past the bend at a 45-degree angle.

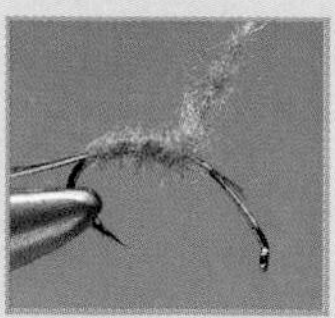

2 Start to form the body with the herl, CDC or other dubbing material.

3 Complete the body. Remove any waste body material and wind the ribbing. Tie in a bunch of peacock herls. How many depends on the size of the fly being tied. On tiny patterns, tie in the butt ends of the guard hairs used for the tails.

4 Strip away the fluff from the base of the hackle and tie in immediately in front of the herls. Dub on the hare's ear fur or chosen thorax material.

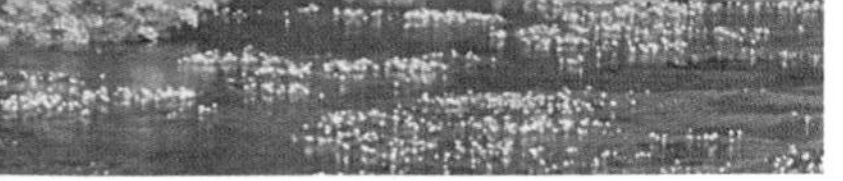

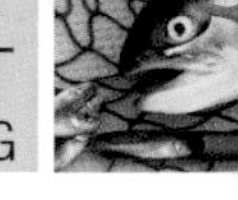

One on an Easy-Peasy USD Dun, which creates a lifelike 'footprint' on the water

5 If a wing is required, tie in the poly yarn to project at 90 degrees to the hook shank. You might find it easier to tie in the wing if the hook is inverted in the vice. Dub on a little more of the thorax material and wind it round the base of the wing to hide the roots. Begin to wind the hackle through the thorax.

6 Finish winding the hackle. Secure and snip away the waste feather. Divide the hackle fibres on the back of the hook and bring the peacock herls over to the eye to form the thorax cover. Trim off the waste herl. Form a small head, whip finish and add a tiny drop of varnish to the head and thorax cover to complete the fly.

EASY-PEASY USD DUN

HOOK: Size 10–16 curved midge or sedge

TAIL: Mink or fox guard hairs

BODY: Herl, CDC or fine dubbing to suit colour of the natural

RIB *(optional)*: Oval gold tinsel

THORAX: Hare's ear fur or fine dubbing

THORAX COVER: Peacock herl

WING *(optional)*: Grey, tan or white poly yarn

HACKLE: Cock hackles, one or two depending on fly size, the colour to match the insect imitated

Queen for a Day

A duck and a wulff for the mayfly carnival

More time with pen and fly-tying vice, more hopes and dreams, have been dedicated to the mayfly than to any other insect. While the season for this most ephemeral of ephemerids is all too short, it manages to capture the imagination of each generation of fly-fishers like no other. As the hatch reaches its peak, great rafts of butter-yellow duns appear as if by magic and it can seem as if every trout in the river has thrown caution to the wind to gorge on this short-lived feast.

Britain has two species, *Ephemera danica* and *Ephemera vulgata*. In size and profile they are almost identical: *E. danica* is the mayfly of the chalk stream and the limestone lake, while the darker, more olive, *E. vulgata* is usually found on slow rivers and small lakes.

CDC MAYFLY
HOOK: Size 8–10
THREAD: Brown
TAIL: A few fibres of deer hair or moose mane
BODY: Cream fur
RIB: Stout brown thread
WING: Natural grey CDC
HACKLE: Grizzle cock

CDC Mayfly

The soft, downy feathers found around the preen gland of various duck species, such as the mallard, make a near-perfect material for the wings of many fly imitations and few more so than those of the mayfly dun. These feathers are better known under the French name, cul-de-canard, or CDC for short.

In the CDC Mayfly pattern, a simple pair of natural grey CDC feathers is used for the wings. When placed back-to-back and positioned sloping back over the body, the wing looks very natural. Choose the largest available with plenty of soft fibres to give the finished wing the correct density.

The CDC Mayfly is tied in a standard dry-fly style. The only minor deviation is that the hackle is applied in open turns over the thorax rather than as a dense ruff. This 'thorax-tie', as it is known, produces a sparser effect and gives a more natural footprint on the water's surface while still being ample to keep the fly floating.

tip

• Trimming away the hackle fibres beneath the fly helps it sit low on the surface.

RELATED SUBJECTS: • Cul-de-canard p38 • Fishing with combinations of flies p104

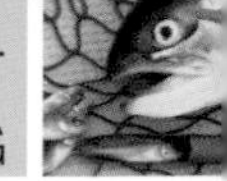

Grey Wulff

Few would deny that Lee Wulff's classic creations rank among the best dry-flies ever devised. In small sizes, they represent a whole host of insects, but when they are dressed big they really come into their own.

When the mayfly is up they are deadly on lakes and rivers, often beating painstakingly devised close-copy imitations by a country mile. The increasing regularity with which they appear in the catch-return books of major English chalk streams proves how effective they are – and only the foolish would dream of going afloat on the great loughs of the Irish west at mayfly time without a Wulff or two in his box.

GREY WULFF
HOOK: Size 8–10
THREAD: Black
TAIL: Grey squirrel tail
BODY: Grey rabbit fur
HACKLE: Blue dun cock
WING: Grey squirrel tail

tip

- Forming a neat head on a fly with prominent head hackles is made easy if a short length of drinking straw is slit down one side and then slipped over the hackle fibres.

Big Summer Sedges

Things that go sploosh in the night

Few things set a fisherman's nerves tingling like the sound of the energetic rise of a large trout to the big sedges of a summer night. Sedges (caddis flies) come in all sizes but some are amongst the largest insects on the water. The trout know this. Adult sedges rarely sit still, skittering across the surface and causing quite a disturbance. Trout know this as well. In defiance of the usual practice of dry-fly fishing, sedge imitations should be moved, a little or a lot, to induce that characteristic, thrilling, slashing rise.

tip

- Both these sedge patterns are normally fished as a single dry-fly but their cork-like qualities can be used to suspend a sedge pupa imitation (or any other nymph) on a length of nylon tied to the bend of the hook (New Zealand style).

Success with the sedge

RELATED SUBJECTS:

- New Zealand style droppers p37 and 53

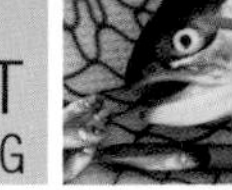

G&H Sedge

G&H SEDGE
HOOK: Size 8–12
THREAD: Green or tan
UNDERBODY: Green seal's fur
BODY: Natural deer hair spun in bunches and clipped to shape
ANTENNAE *(optional)*: Stripped hackle stalks

The G&H Sedge is the best known of all John Goddard's many innovative flies. The deer-hair bodied dry-fly floats like a cork and is regarded as the premier sedge imitation in America where it is better known as the Goddard Caddis.

It was devised in collaboration with the late Cliff Henry – hence the G&H. Their idea was to come up with a fly that, when seen from beneath, provided the distinctive wedge-shaped silhouette. Keep this feeding trigger in mind when shaving the ragged bundle of spun deer hair into its final shape.

It was originally intended to represent the mottled sedge, but by matching the size of the artificial to that of the hatching insect, the G&H can be used to represent any of the lighter sedges. By substituting a dark brown seal's fur underbody for the original green and using a darker deer hair, the G&H can be adapted for use in cases where brown or near-black sedges are plentiful.

tip

- To avoid the fly being 'bounced' rather than firmly taken by the rising trout, all the deer hair fibres must be trimmed from beneath the shank so that the hook stands proud of the body.

Elk Hair Sedge

The Elk Hair Sedge, originated by Al Troth, has become a standard dry-fly on British waters. It is not difficult to see why, as it imitates a small- to medium-sized adult sedge superbly.

Shape and buoyancy are just right and, even on fast broken water, it bobs along on the surface like the proverbial cork. When required, it can be skated across the surface, the stiff hackle points simulating the legs of a freshly hatched sedge fly.

Like so many top-rate patterns, it is both robust and reasonably easy to tie. It also uses readily available materials in its construction, hare's fur and elk hair. The elk hair gives it a lifelike profile and some natural buoyancy.

The Elk Hair Sedge will work on any river or stream where sedge flies of various species are found. It works best on fast- to medium-paced water, especially where the surface is broken. Sedges usually hatch and lay eggs in the late afternoon through into dark and this is when the Elk Hair Sedge is at its most effective. Give it a little twitch as it drifts downstream to induce a slashing rise.

ELK HAIR SEDGE
HOOK: Size 10–14 down-eyed, medium weight
THREAD: Red
RIB: Fine gold wire
BODY: Hare's fur
BODY HACKLE: Furnace cock hackle
WING: Natural elk hair or bleached elk hock

• Controlling deer hair p65
• Spinning deer hair p104

Big and Bouncy

Hunky, high-riders born on the brawling waters of the American west

There are times and places where the water is so turbulent as to drown all but the biggest, most buoyant dry flies. This is the time to bring on the creations in deer hair and foam. These flies, originally tied for the big waters of the Rocky Mountains, are virtually unsinkable They are also large enough to be visible by fish and fishermen in the maelstrom of white water rivers.

Then again there are times when the trout are engrossed in feeding on something so small it is difficult or impossible to imitate with a normal fly. This can be the time to offer them something so large and insistent that even the most fastidious feeder just cannot let it pass downstream. Hans van Klinken's original Klinkhamer did just this: in sizes 8 and 10, it dwarfed the usual flies, real and artificial, that trout were accustomed to (see pages 36–37). A daddy-long-legs can be used in this role but there are things larger and louder that seem to shock the trout out of their preoccupation if dropped lightly on their noses.

tips

- Big flies need big leaders as they can helicopter in a wind, twisting light leaders into knots.
- Big fish are attracted to these meaty mouthfuls. Be prepared for smash takes.

Fishing a 'bouncy' mountain river

RELATED SUBJECT:

- New Zealand style droppers pp37 and 50

With a small selection of these meaty and buoyant patterns, the angler is prepared for both of these situations.

Curiously, the Humpy and Stimulator are especially effective during the mayfly hatch, often out-fishing more slavish imitations.

Humpy

HUMPY
HOOK: Size 4–12
THREAD: To match body colour
TAIL AND WING: Moose or deer hair
BODY: Yellow, olive or red floss
HACKLE: Brown and grizzle cock hackles wound together

Reams of deer hair make this fly virtually unsinkable. Perfect for boisterous rapids at the head of a pool. Trout have little option but to commit, so expect confident takes. A bright red body is a favourite with Irish anglers at mayfly time.

The Stimulator

This is usually used as a single fly but its built-in buoyancy can also be used to support one or two nymphs strung, New Zealand style, from the bend of the hook. The Stimulator is great in hatches of sedges and surprisingly good on chalk streams in a mayfly hatch.

THE STIMULATOR
HOOK: Size 6–10
THREAD: Orange tail elk hair
BODY: Orange, cream, tan and green seal's fur or polypropylene dubbing
WING: Elk hair
BODY HACKLE: Furnace cock
THORAX: Amber seal's fur
HACKLE: Grizzle cock

Chernobyl Ant

A truly monstrous thing. In smaller sizes this is a great fly to fish on rain-fed rivers. By using different colours of foam for sighting wings, one of them will be seen whatever the light conditions. Extend the foam well over the hook bend and eye.

CHERNOBYL ANT
HOOK: Size 8–10
THREAD: Yellow
BODY: Black foam over tan foam
LEGS: Black rubber
SIGHTING WINGS: Two slips of foam

Stillwater

Fly-fishing for trout in lakes has roots in two very different traditions

Scotland, Ireland and Wales have many hundreds of large lochs, loughs and llyns, fed by clean, rocky streams draining the surrounding hills. Native brown trout have spawned in these streams since the last ice age. The trout parr slip down the streams into the large lakes where they can graze and grow on the abundant insects.

In Ireland and Scotland in particular, these waters can be very large, allowing formidable waves to build up under a strong wind, particularly when that wind is funnelling down the glacial valleys of the Highlands or pushing straight in from the Atlantic on the west coast of Ireland. A variety of long-keeled, seaworthy boat – and a breed of professional boatmen – has evolved on these waters to cope with these conditions. With them has evolved a style of fly-fishing for the indigenous brown trout. The boat drifts side-on to the wind with the angler or anglers casting a short floating line with three, sometimes four, flies ahead of the boat. The rod is raised as the boat drifts towards the flies, allowing the nearest fly to fuss in the surface as for long as possible before the cast is rolled forward again. Boat and flies are always on the move across the surface.

England has no large natural trout waters outside the Lake District. Throughout the 20th century many reservoirs, large and small, were built to cope with an increasing demand for water from growing conurbations and industry. Many of these became renowned trout fisheries with huge growth rates and prodigious catches in the early years. These reservoirs, now mature lakes, are stocked with hatchery-reared rainbow trout and (to a lesser extent) brown trout. The style of fishing on these reservoirs reflects these differences (see pages 78–99). The margins of most reservoirs are accessible and bank-fishing is usual. Drift-fishing is less suitable on some of the smaller waters, and under more benign weather conditions, anchoring and casting from a fixed position is more common. The hothouse of competition fishing and the stillwater-trout boom of the 1970s and 1980s resulted in an astonishing evolution of techniques – and flies.

Drifters and Squatters

Stocked rainbows and wild browns - and the anglers who pursue them - have very different approaches to feeding and fishing

Stillwater trout

The principal difference between wild brown trout and rainbows, from an angling perspective, is that browns are largely territorial fish and rainbows like to shoal-up and wander. Traditional boat-fishing – drifting the shallows, working along a contour line, and continually covering new 'ground' – reflects the territorial behaviour of wild trout. The modern reservoir tactic of anchoring the boat is suited to rainbow-trout behaviour. This modern tactic is hopeless for the large majority of wild brown trout populations because, once an area has been fished for a given amount of time, the trout within it are either caught or spooked. The alternative reservoir technique of finding a bank location and staying put is not suitable for brown trout for exactly the same reason.

Wild brown trout inhabit a three-dimensional territory, reaching from loch bed to surface. Their hunting technique tends to be in a vertical direction, the fish lying deep and feeding above their position. Rainbow trout (and stocked brown trout) move in shoals and tend to feed in a horizontal direction, feeding at a given depth and continually moving throughout this horizontal plane in search of new food items.

Rainbows are pelagic feeders, like other shoaling species. They are much more selective feeders than wild browns, often concentrating on one specific item of prey abundant at a specific depth, with few opportunistic additions. Finding this depth – and this prey item – is the key to catching stocked trout.

Wild brown trout spend their early years in streams, occupying individual territories (lies) and feeding on whatever the current brings them. Their adult feeding mirrors this lifestyle. They feed primarily in an area that provides their day-to-day requirements. As a result, wild brown trout tend to show a greater variety of prey in stomach-content analysis.

Brown trout feeding behaviour

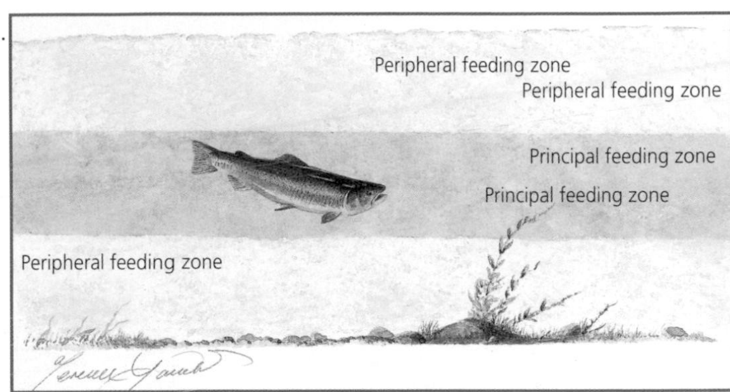

Rainbow trout feeding behaviour

Of course, in life nothing is that simple. There are several populations of wild trout that show pelagic behaviour. Ireland's Lough Melvin produces large quantities of daphnia. A population of wild brown trout, known locally as sonaghan, has adopted a pelagic lifestyle to exploit this rich resource and has evolved into a distinct sub-species, not interbreeding with other races of trout in the lough. Other lochs show a similar, if watered-down, version of this phenomenon.

How does this affect the fisherman after wild brown trout? His tactics should be shaped to suit the fish. Boat-drifting the shallows and step-and-cast wading are by far the best means to locate larger wild trout. Brown trout are territorial, opportunistic feeders. Offer them variety in fly selection: this will mimic the natural diversity of food items entering their domain. The bulk of natural feed is found in shallow water so concentrate your efforts there – it's where the bulk of fish – and every glass-case specimen – will be.

If you are on a loch where the locals fish over deep, open water, be assured that trout with a pelagic lifestyle are to be found there and reservoir techniques will catch them. Carry a variety of line densities as depth can be critical. More than likely the fish will be feeding on daphnia, and flies in black, white, orange or lime-green are likely to do the business.

Loch, Llyn and Lough

Wild brown trout in natural lakes

The wild trout lakes of the British Isles are all in regions where salmon is the angler's greatest prize and trout fishing was – perhaps still is – something the fisherman did while the salmon fishing was out of sorts. In the fishier bits of Scotland and Ireland 'a fish' still means a salmon.

Enthusiastic trout are taken on salmon flies when drifting a loch, just as salmon will take a fly intended for trout. As a consequence, traditional loch trout flies in these regions were often scaled-down and simplified versions of the local full-dressed salmon flies. There is a certain irony in this: the original salmon flies were almost certainly scaled-up versions of the patterns tied for trout at a time before fly-fishing for salmon was thought worthwhile.

These traditional patterns often feature the by-products of the sporting life in these upland regions: feathers of mallard, grouse, pheasant and partridge, and the fur of hare. Trout flies were fished on a floating line and mimicked life in the upper layers, with large wings and palmered or dubbed bodies a recurrent feature. These bedraggled flies work best in the big wave of a large loch where many of the natural flies end up in a similar state.

The growth of stocked fisheries has had a profound effect on the fishing of these wild natural waters. Fishermen who learned to fish on English reservoirs, using flylines of different densities, heavily weighted flies, prodigious leaders and indicators, can sometimes catch fish when the traditional methods falter or fail. Local fishermen have not been slow to borrow ideas from the visitors. Nor to adapt some of their dressings to include iridescent plastics and fluorescent colours.

Duckfly

Combine ancient and modern for the midge of wilder waters

Whatever you call them – buzzers, chironomids or duckflies – they're all midges, and all taste the same to a trout whether it swims in a great lough of Ireland's far west, a Welsh llyn, or a little lochan hidden away in the Scottish highlands.

In Ireland they are known as duckflies and can be so prolific that they lift off the water like a swirl of smoke. Irish anglers accord them almost equal status with the meaty mayfly – and the great trout of the limestone loughs would agree.

English buzzer imitations were developed on the benign waters of the southern reservoirs where the teams of slim flies were fished almost static to intercept the roving shoals of rainbows. It is not a method suited to the wilder, windier waters of the great Irish loughs in a spring blow. Irish duckflies bristle with movement. They are fished close to the surface where there is wave movement to work the mobile hackles.

The Snatcher was invented to imitate the large buzzers hatching on Loch Leven. It uses the slim, curved profile of the Irish duckfly but adds a palmered hackle to emphasize the movement of a pupa struggling to

DOOBRY SNATCHER

HOOK: **Size 10–14 Kamasan B100**

THREAD: **Brown or red**

TAG: **Orange fluorescent floss – Glo Brite no. 4**

RIB: **Fine gold wire**

BODY: **Flat gold Mylar tinsel**

BODY HACKLE: **Black cock hackle**

COLLAR HACKLE: **Dyed-orange hen badger**

CHEEKS: **Jungle cock**

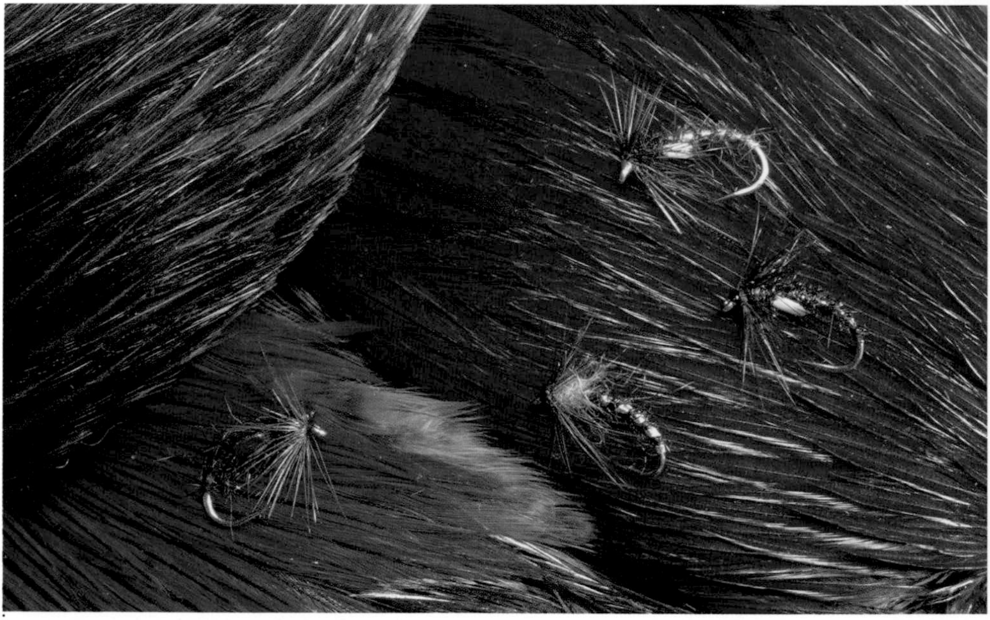

A selection of Snatchers against a hackle cape

TYING THE DOOBRY SNATCHER

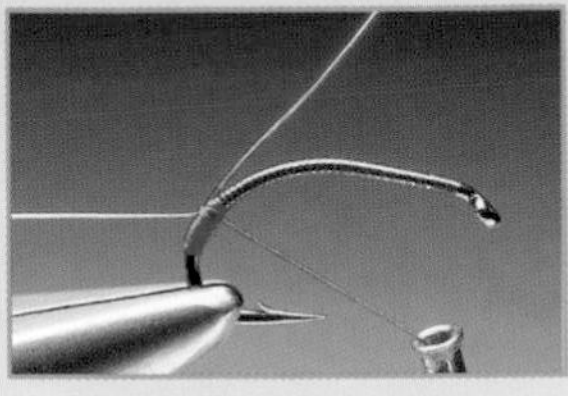

1 Build a short tag with the floss. Run on normal brown tying thread and catch in 2in of fine gold wire.

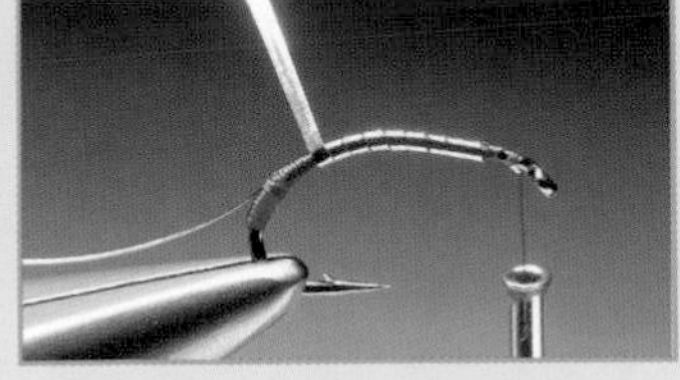

2 Wind the tying thread over the hook and the wire. Catch in a 3in length of gold Mylar tinsel just short of the eye. Take hold of the Mylar tinsel and wind it along the shank in close turns. Don't overlap the turns.

3 Wind the tinsel to the tag then back to the catching-in point. Secure the end and trim. Catch in a dyed-black cock hackle with a fibre length one-and-a-half times that of the hook gape. Wind it down the body to the tag in evenly spaced turns.

4 Keeping tension on the hackle, begin winding the gold wire up through it, locking the hackle in place. Secure the wire at the eye and trim wire and hackle tip. Catch in a dyed-orange hen badger hackle at the eye.

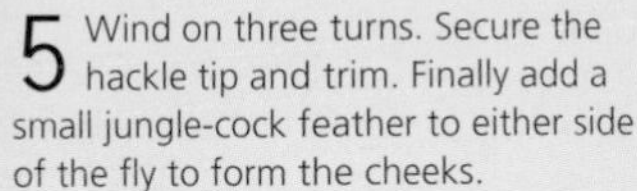

5 Wind on three turns. Secure the hackle tip and trim. Finally add a small jungle-cock feather to either side of the fly to form the cheeks.

hatch near the surface. It was so successful that the same Snatcher treatment was applied to established wet-fly patterns such as Bibio, Blue Zulu and Claret Bumble.

This, the Doobry version, is based on a Stan Headley pattern and has the same black, gold and orange combination.

The key to the Snatcher's success is the curved profile along with its palmered body hackle, which works beautifully in the water. This hackle should not be applied too heavily.

The original didn't have cheeks but these have become standard, using either dyed goose biots or jungle cock. The cheeks are small, to suggest the wing buds of an emerging fly.

BLACK DUCKFLY
HOOK: Size 8–14 curved grub
THREAD: Black
BODY: Black seal's fur
RIB: Silver holographic tinsel
THORAX: Grey seal's fur
CHEEKS: Jungle cock
HACKLE: Grey dyed badger

The Mayfly

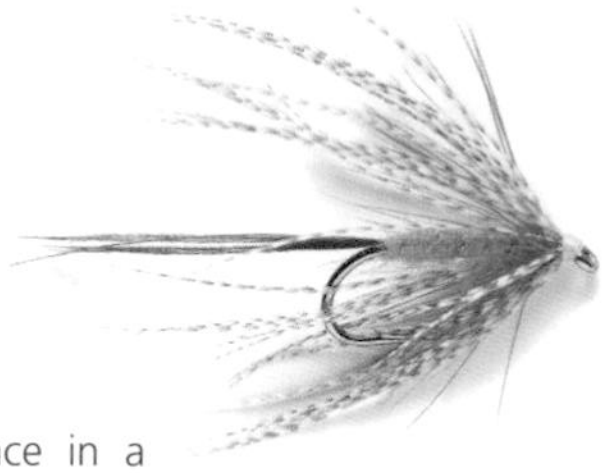

It can be the highlight of the fishing year – and a source of fascination and frustration

The annual festival of the mayfly takes place on mature stillwaters of all kinds from lowland reservoirs to Highland lochs, beginning in May and stretching into the first weeks of June. Just how important this hatch is to the resident fish and fishermen depends on the density of the hatch. On a stony, acid lochan only the occasional mayfly will hatch and, like as not, will be ignored by the trout. On richer waters these meaty insects can hatch in incredible numbers, and large trout which lurk unsuspected in the depths throughout the year may throw caution to the wind and come up to the surface in a gluttonous carnival.

This carnival reaches its apogee on the great limestone loughs in the west of Ireland, and fishermen from around the world make an annual pilgrimage to take part.

Wind, waves and weather will determine the way the fish come to the feast – and what the angler must offer the fish. The best trout could be concentrating on the hatching nymphs, the newly emerged duns riding the waves, or the dying adults, spent with mating and egg-laying and now lying feebly in the surface.

GOSLING

HOOK: Size 8–10 longshank

THREAD: Yellow

TAIL: Cock pheasant tail fibres

BODY: Yellow seal's fur

RIB: Oval gold tinsel

HACKLE: Speckled grey mallard flank feather over orange cock hackle

Boat-fishing on an Irish lough

RELATED SUBJECT:

• Avoid helicoptering p71

1 Run the tying thread down to the bend in close turns. Catch in three or four fibres of cock pheasant tail and 3in of fine silver wire. Take the tying thread back up the shank covering the waste ends of the wire and pheasant tail fibres. Take a pinch of white deer hair and catch it in so that its tips project just past the hook bend.

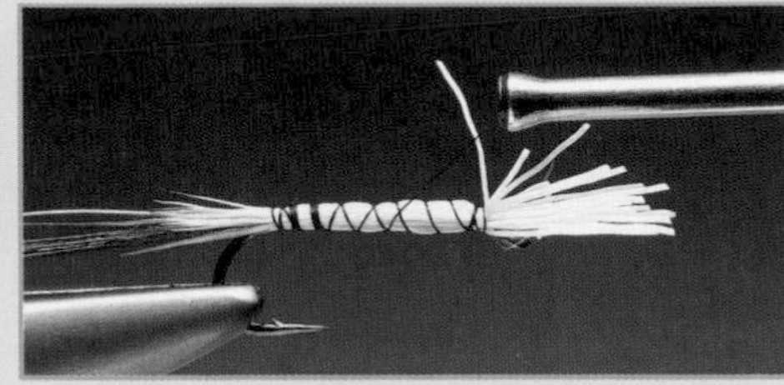

2 Position the deer hair along the hook shank. Wind the tying thread over it in open, evenly spaced turns. Don't pull the thread too tight. Make a few close turns near the tail to mimic the markings of the natural. Wind back to the head to form a criss-cross pattern. Now wind the silver wire over the body in evenly spaced turns. This adds protection to the soft deer hair.

3 Trim hair stubs. Catch in a long-fibred black cock hackle. Wind on five or six turns and secure. Trim the hackle fibres short to form the thorax.

4 Take a long-fibred brown hackle and catch it in at the eye. Wind on five or six turns. Position the fibres either side with figure-of-eight thread wraps to form the spent wings.

In a good wind and wave the Irish tradition is to dap a pair of the natural insects or to work a team of bedraggled wet-flies through the surface. The Gosling and its variations are local favourites.

In light winds and sparse hatches it may be more profitable to put on a dry-fly and target individual rising fish. Be patient: a good fish will stay within a small territory and a large dry-fly is best left to fish without drag. The Grey Wulff is a reliable performer (see page 49).

It is harder to spot when the best trout have switched to mopping up the spent adults, lying in the surface film. Only a close copy of this 'spent gnat' will serve now. The Deerstalker is a superb imitation.

DEERSTALKER

HOOK: Size 10 longshank

THREAD: Black or brown

TAIL: Cock pheasant tail fibres

RIB: Tying thread and fine silver wire

BODY: White deer hair

THORAX: Black cock hackle wound and clipped short

WING: Long-fibred furnace cock hackle

Fluttering Sedges

Things that go 'buzz' in the night

Sedges (adult caddis flies) form the basis of many traditional Irish lough flies. The Green Peter and its many derivatives are modelled on a natural sedge of the same name. There are over 200 species in Britain, in all sizes from tiny to titanic, but most are in shades of brown.

Fish will take adult sedges both when they hatch out on the surface and again when they return to lay their eggs. Adult sedges rarely sit still, constantly skittering across the surface and causing quite a disturbance. Sedge imitations mimic this with a palmered or heavily dubbed body to give the fly 'fuzz'. The illusion is completed by skating the fly across the surface or giving it an occasional twitch. The larger species usually hatch in high summer towards dusk and into a warm night. This is exciting fishing, casting into the gloom and listening – rather than looking – for those great, splashy rises.

The Sedgehog

This is an adaptation, by Stan Headley, of an original pattern by Orkney angler and fly-tyer Sandy Nicholson. Although first intended as a buoyant wet-fly, it soon proved to be a worthy imitation of a range of small to medium-sized sedges.

It can be tied in a variety of body colours including the claret seal's fur, which is used here. In every one, however, the wing is the same and is formed by layering bunches of deer hair tips. The

Sedges are easily recognized by their roof-shaped wings

SEDGEHOG
HOOK: Size 10–14 wet-fly
THREAD: Black or brown
TAIL: Bunch of deer hair tips
BODY: Claret seal's fur, applied in sections
WING: Bunches of dark deer hair
HACKLE: Light brown cock hackle

mottled hairs make a great imitation of the wing of the natural sedge, while their buoyancy helps the fly to float even when it is twitched across the surface to imitate the action of the freshly hatched fly.

When tying this style of wing it is important to control the hair. As it is applied, firm thread wraps are used to lock it in position while the fingers prevent the bunch from spinning around the shank. Once securely in place, looser turns are made around the base to ensure that the bunch sits low and doesn't flare too much.

TYING THE SEDGEHOG

1 Run the tying thread down to the bend in touching turns. Take a bunch of well-marked deer-hair fibres, ensuring that the tips are level. Using tight turns of thread, fix the deer hair in place so that the tips project past the bend to form the tail.

2 Wind a few softer, looser turns back along the tail. These softer turns will control the hair and stop it flaring out of place. Remove excess hair.

3 Dub on a generous pinch of claret seal's fur to produce a thick rope and wind the fur over the base of the tail, making the first turn quite soft so that the deer hair, again, doesn't flare.

4 Take a second bunch of deer hair and position it in front of those of the tail, secure and wind on more dubbing.

5 Repeat this until the entire shank has been covered. On a hook of this size three of each is about right

6 Remove the hair stubs and tie in a brown cock hackle. Wind on three full turns. Secure the hackle tip and finish with a small, neat head. Finally trim away the hackle fibres beneath the hook.

MURROUGH
HOOK: Size 8–10 longshank
THREAD: Brown
RIB: Oval gold tinsel
BODY: Claret seal's fur
WING: Brown turkey
HACKLE: Brown cock hackle
ANTENNAE: Cock pheasant tail fibres

The Murrough

For the huge sedge of summer, try the Murrough – the Great Red Sedge *(right)*. Skitter it across the surface at dusk and be prepared for some crashing takes.

Colours To Dye For

Indian cock capes come in every natural shade imaginable and, once dipped into a bright dye, the colour combinations are amazing. Achieving a particular colour isn't difficult – if certain rules are followed to the letter. As ever, practice makes perfect so, before you move on to the more expensive capes, it's best to experiment with cheap ones.

A white cape has been transformed into subtle shades of fiery brown (right) - superb for Irish lough flies

DYEING A FIERY BROWN CAPE

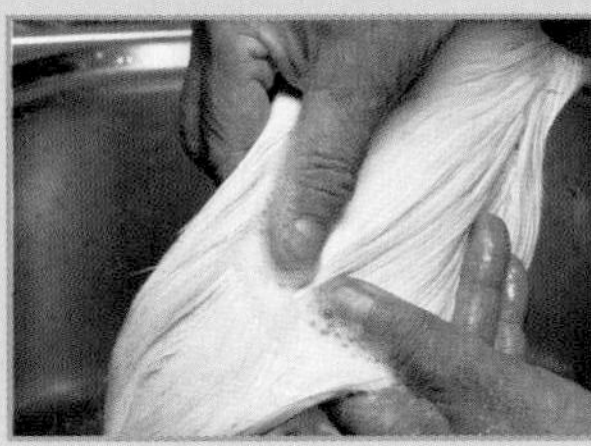

1 Every vestige of grease must be removed from the cape using Venpol or a similar degreaser if the subsequent steps are to be successful. Rinse well after an hour.

2 Wearing gloves, add a carefully measured amount of dye to the hot water, following the packet instructions for quantities. Add a tablespoon of vinegar to fix the dye.

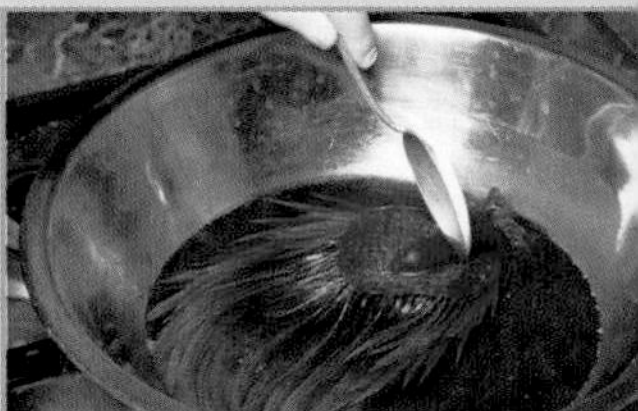

3 The cape must be completely immersed. Agitate to ensure the dye reaches every part of it.

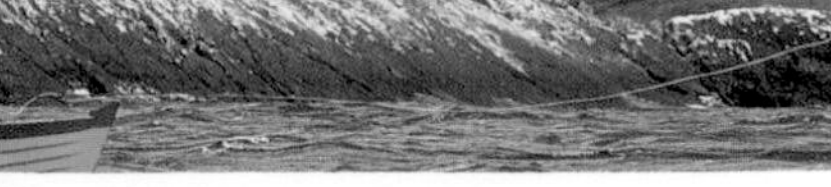

tips

- Thoroughly degrease the fur or feathers to be dyed in a solution of Venpol and hand-hot water in a vessel big enough to take all the material. Immerse the material and move it around in the water for a few minutes. Agitate again after 30 minutes. Wash off the solution with hot water after an hour.
- Mix the dye powder with a small amount of hot water and make up to the full volume once the dye is completely dissolved.
- Keep the dye bath at an even temperature: as hot as the hand will stand and no hotter.
- Handle the dry powder with great care.
- Always prepare the materials for the dye bath in a sink.
- Work in an area that can be easily cleaned or a place where dye spillage doesn't matter.
- Remove the cape from the dye bath frequently and examine under natural light, always bearing in mind the fact that feathers appear darker when wet.
- When the correct shade is reached, wash off the excess dye. Do not squeeze it too hard and never wring it out. Pat the cape dry between sheets of absorbent paper and finish with a hair-dryer.
- Remember that you can only work from light to dark colours and not the other way around.
- Practise only on cheap capes and feathers.
- Take a sample of the dry feather that has dyed successfully and stick it in a notebook with a record of exactly what you did to achieve that colour, particularly noting length of immersion.

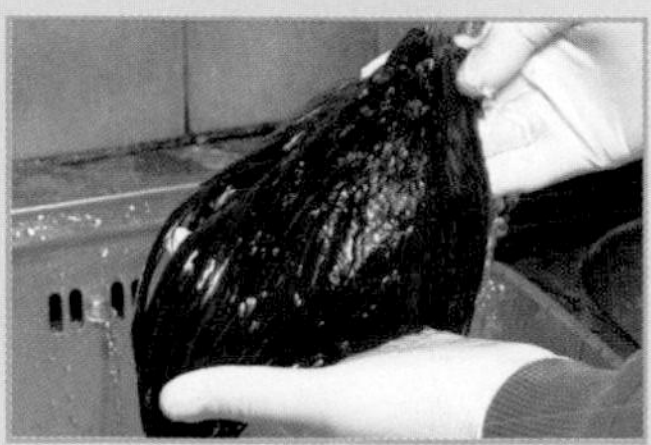

4 Wash the cape under cold running water. The wet cape will be much darker than when it is dry. Remove excess water by gently patting the cape with absorbent paper.

5 A hair-dryer on a low setting speeds up the drying and reveals the cape's true colour.

Bugs and Beetles

Trout are always ready for a meal dropping in

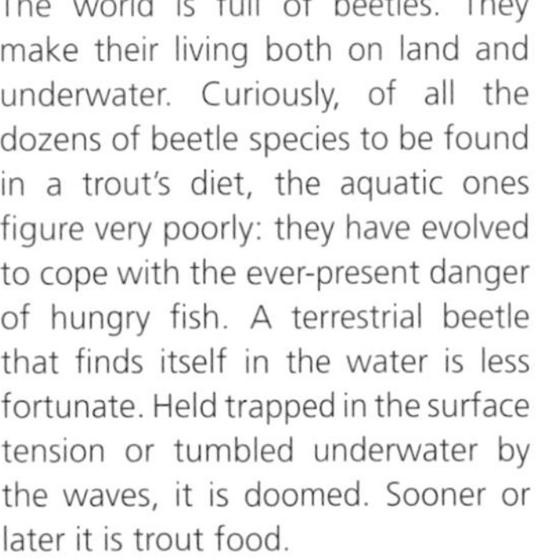

The world is full of beetles. They make their living both on land and underwater. Curiously, of all the dozens of beetle species to be found in a trout's diet, the aquatic ones figure very poorly: they have evolved to cope with the ever-present danger of hungry fish. A terrestrial beetle that finds itself in the water is less fortunate. Held trapped in the surface tension or tumbled underwater by the waves, it is doomed. Sooner or later it is trout food.

Some beetles arrive on the water in prodigious numbers. The most famous of all is the coch-y-bondhu, the small garden chafer, otherwise known as the bracken clock. It is about half an inch long with reddish-brown wing cases and a metallic bluish-green thorax and head. It is common in many grassy uplands of Wales and Scotland and during early summer appears in large numbers, when it is capable of inducing a dramatic rise among wild trout.

The coch-y-bondhu tends to fly during the warmest part of the day and when it is blown on to the water the surface quickly becomes dotted with rising trout.

Terrestrial beetles float very low on the surface, so the most effective imitations should sit in the same position. Buoyant materials like deer hair and foam have been used to create lifelike floating imitations but the traditional wet-fly patterns remain remarkably effective when the fish are feeding beneath the surface.

FOAM BEETLE

HOOK: Size 12–16

THREAD: Black

BODY: Peacock herl

BACK: Black microcellular foam

HACKLE: Dyed-black cock hackle

ANTENNAE: Two strands of dyed-black deer hair

TYING THE FOAM BEETLE

1 Take the thread to a point opposite the barb. Holding the foam on the top of the hook, secure the foam with tight turns of thread.

2 Trim off the delicate ends from a pair of peacock herls and catch them in. Twist the herls into a rope and begin to form the body.

3 Complete the body and trim waste herls. Add the two black deer-hair fibres to represent the antennae.

4 Catch in the cock hackle, wind on two turns and secure. Bring the foam over the herl body, forcing the upward-pointing hackle fibres to the flanks.

5 Cut away the unwanted foam to leave a small stub pointing out over the hook eye. Use a whip finish to secure the foam in place.

RELATED SUBJECT:

• Reinforcing peacock herl p99

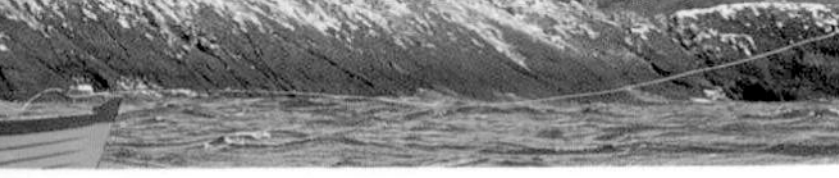

tip

- As beetles are solid creatures, the trout sees them in silhouette, dark against the sky as they float on the surface. Hence the same pattern will serve for beetles of most colours.

COCH-Y-BONDHU BEETLE

The traditional Welsh pattern can be used as a wet-fly or treated with floatant and fished in the surface. It is a great search pattern on small streams during the summer when all manner of bugs can find their way on to the water.

HOOK: **Size 12–14**

THREAD: **Crimson**

TAG: **Flat gold tinsel**

BODY: **Peacock herl**

HACKLE: **Light furnace hackle**

Coch-y-bondhu beetles are a terrestrial treat for wild trout

All Arms and Legs

The daddy-long-legs is a huge, helpless meal for a hungry trout

The daddy-long-legs, or crane-fly, is another land-born insect that provides an important part of the trout's diet at specific times of the year. Daddies are not strong fliers and a stiff offshore breeze will see large numbers blown on to the water. They seem quite at home at first, sitting comfortably with legs outstretched on the water. They are even able to take flight, hopping along as they are blown downwind – an action perfectly mimicked with the dapped fly. But eventually they become swamped and trout will gorge with gusto.

The occasional daddy-long-legs can be seen at any time but it is not until the cooler, damper conditions of autumn that there are sufficient numbers about to fascinate the fish. This doesn't mean, though, that fishing an imitation works only at the back end. Curiously, at times where there is little noticeable surface activity, a dry Daddy can be successful on river or lake, especially when other methods have failed (see page 52).

When the first major falls begin it takes a while for the fish to tune in, possibly because it is such a large insect. However, when they do, dry-fly fishing with a good imitation can be both dramatic and effective, especially on stillwaters. On the large Irish loughs the live insect is one of the great dapping baits and a big artificial Daddy can be even better. While it is possible to get some good fishing to the Daddy on reservoirs, it is on the natural lakes and loughs where they make a significant contribution to the fishing calendar. At such times a good pattern with those all-important trailing legs can work very well indeed, fished either dry or wet.

fishing with daddy

- Though six legs are the standard for an insect imitation, adding an extra two doesn't put the fish off and it does make the fly last longer.
- Daddies are large, wind-resistant flies and have a tendency to helicopter when cast. Use a stout leader, 6-8lb, to minimize the problem.
- Missed takes and precarious hook-hold are a frustrating hazard when dapping, particularly when using artificial flies. One solution is to tie a chunky daddy-long-legs as a tube fly. Slide the fly up the dapping leader and arm the end with a size 14 or 16 treble hook.

DRY DADDY

HOOK: Size 10 longshank
THREAD: Brown
RIB: Clear nylon mono
BODY: Tan SLF (Synthetic Living Fibre) dubbing
LEGS: Knotted fibres of cock pheasant tail
THORAX: Tan SLF
WING: Grizzle hackles
HACKLE: Furnace cock

WET DADDY

HOOK: Size 10 longshank
THREAD: Brown
RIB: Gold wire
BODY: Light brown floss
LEGS: Knotted fibres of cock pheasant tail
HACKLE: Light brown cock, tied long

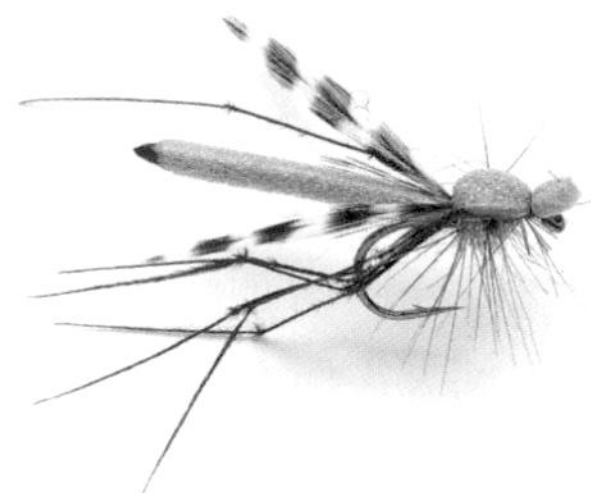

FOAM DADDY

HOOK: Size 10
THREAD: Brown
BODY: Light brown foam strip burnt at one end
THORAX: Hare's fur under light brown foam
LEGS: Knotted fibres of cock pheasant tail
WING: Grizzle cock hackles
HACKLE: Ginger cock

Bumbles

Light through a kaleidoscope of colours

Derbyshire anglers relied on them for centuries, Halford had great faith in them for both trout and grayling, and Justice Kingsmill Moore's inspired tinkering with them ensured them an everlasting place in fly-fishing history. It would be a rare cast on an Irish lough that had no room for one of these extravagantly hackled wet-flies.

Not only did the late judge give us the dressings of some of the most deadly flies ever devised, he went to great lengths to describe not only the specific colours that should be used in their dressing but why they played such an important role.

He stressed that his own Bumbles, compared to the opaque and immaculately dressed English lake flies, were tied in such a way that the light passed through the hackles to be reflected from the tinsel buried deep in the tangle of seal's fur and therefore turn the body into a haze of subtle hues.

No other form of fly-tying creates such translucence, and the hackles, especially those that have been carefully dyed, take on an internal fire and sparkle that changes with every twist and turn of the fly to create a shifting illusion of life. Kingsmill Moore suggested that the choice of colours and materials depended solely on the skill of the tyer. He was convinced of the importance of the quality of materials and of the seal's fur in particular.

Kingsmill Moore claimed that, because of their innate translucency, the Bumbles were at their most deadly when drawn through the surface, or close to it and observed by the trout from underneath. Sound enough reason why dropper flies should be translucent while those chosen for the tail should be opaque.

Of all the Bumbles, the Golden Olive Bumble is probably the most popular. Suggesting everything from olives to sedges, it can be used at any time of the season with complete confidence. Dressed on a size 10 hook, it can be a deadly fly to use at mayfly time.

GOLDEN OLIVE BUMBLE

HOOK: Size 8–14

THREAD: Brown

TAIL: Golden pheasant crest feather

RIB: Fine oval gold tinsel

BODY: Golden-olive seal's fur

HACKLE: Red game and golden olive

COLLAR HACKLE: Blue jay fibres

TYING THE GOLDEN OLIVE BUMBLE

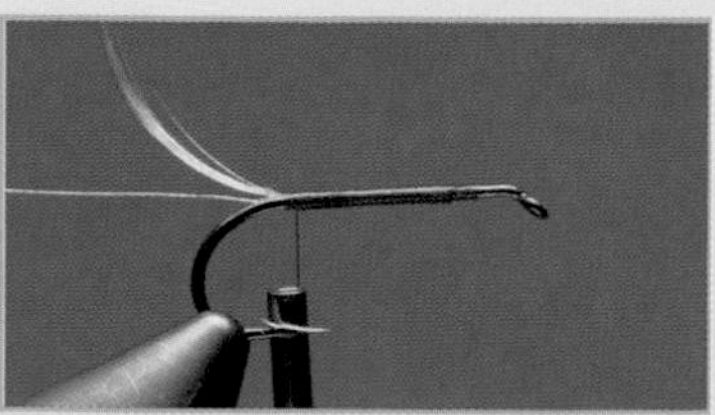

1 Flatten the stem of a golden pheasant crest feather with forceps or pliers. Tie in as a tail. Secure the gold tinsel rib at the same point. For neatness and security, the tinsel should run almost the whole length of the body.

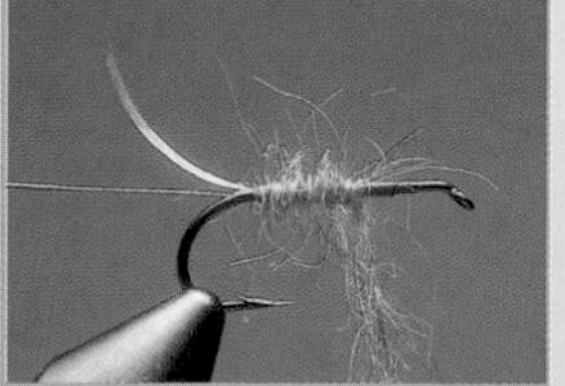

2 Dub on the seal's fur and form a level body. Remove any waste fur from the thread.

3 Strip away the fluff from the base of the hackle feathers and secure them in with several tight turns of thread. Wind the hackle through the seal's fur body in even turns.

RELATED SUBJECTS: • Jay hackles p74 • Shielding hackles p49

4 Wind the hackles to the tail and then wind the ribbing through the hackle in even turns. Secure the rib in front of the hackle and trim away the waste tinsel.

5 With a sharp blade, make a small nick at the top of the blue jay feather and gently tease away the blue side of the feather. If the quill starts to split, encourage it to run in the desired direction with a touch of the blade.

6 Tie in the jay quill and wind it very carefully to form an even collar. Form a small head, whip finish and add a tiny drop of varnish to complete the Golden Olive Bumble.

Six of the Best

Tried and trusted traditional patterns for trout in loch, llyn or lough

Casting for trout

Perhaps the best credential for any fly is that fishermen have relied on it to take trout for many, many years. These patterns – or ones very similar – have stood this test of time on wild trout waters throughout the British Isles. The traditional method is a team of three flies, spaced 3–4 feet apart and fished on a floating or intermediate line. Years ago this would have been achieved by greasing or degreasing a silk line.

With a combination of, say, the Black Pennel on the point, a Silver Invicta on the middle dropper and a Zulu on the top dropper, an angler could fish any loch, llyn or lough with total confidence – which is more important than any choice of fly.

another way with jay

- To form a perfect jay hackle, strip the blue fibres away from the quill and tie them in, facing over the hook eye like an umbrella. Trim the butts and bind down. Now start tying the fly. When the rest of the fly is completed, the jay fibres are drawn back and the head formed.

BLACK PENNEL

HOOK: Size 8–14

THREAD: Black

TAG: Silver tinsel

TAIL: Golden pheasant tippets

BODY: Black floss

RIB: Fine oval silver tinsel

HACKLE: Black cock hackle

SILVER INVICTA

HOOK: Size 8–14

THREAD: Brown

TAIL: Golden pheasant topping

BODY: Silver Mylar tinsel

BODY HACKLE: Palmered brown cock

RIB: Fine silver tinsel

HACKLE: Blue jay throat

WING: Hen pheasant centre tail

KATE MACLAREN

HOOK: Size 8–12

THREAD: Black

TAIL: Golden pheasant topping

BODY: Black seal's fur

BODY HACKLE: Black cock hackle

RIB: Oval silver tinsel

HACKLE: Brown cock hackle

FIERY BROWN

HOOK: Size 8–14

THREAD: Brown

TAIL: Golden pheasant tippets

BODY: Fiery brown seal's fur

RIB: Fine oval gold tinsel

HACKLE: Fiery brown cock throat

WING: Bronze mallard

ZULU

HOOK: Size 8–14

THEAD: Black

TAIL: Red wool or ibis

BODY: Black seal's fur or dyed ostrich herl

BODY HACKLE: Black cock hackle

RIB: Fine silver tinsel

HACKLE: Black cock or hen

BIBIO

HOOK: Size 8–14

THREAD: Black

BODY: Black and hot orange or red seal's fur

BODY HACKLE: Black cock hackle

RIB: Fine oval silver tinsel

HACKLE: Black cock hackle

Dabbling Ducks

A cloak of mallard feather is the secret of this fly for the wind and waves

The Bumble and the Dabbler are the two most popular families of flies on the big wild trout loughs of Ireland. The Bumble (see pages 72–3) is a translucent creature of colour and light. The Dabbler is a more solid affair, suggesting a meaty meal for big fish. This is the product of its characteristic cloak of bronze mallard wing. The long fibres, twisting this way and that in the wave tops, suggest a thoroughly helpless and bedraggled insect. They are at their most bedraggled as the fly is drawing through the surface – dabbling, in fact – and the longer the fisherman can keep it doing just that, the better.

Like many of the great patterns, the Dabbler is effective in a vast range of colours. Its shape and behaviour are its critical virtues. The enfolding wing of bronze mallard fibres is the hallmark of the Dabbler.

DABBLER

HOOK: Size 8–12 heavyweight wet-fly

THREAD: Brown

TAIL: Cock pheasant tail fibres

RIB: Oval gold tinsel

BODY: Golden-olive seal's fur or substitute

WING: Bronze mallard

HACKLE: Brown cock

tips

- A wonderful fly for any large natural lake, especially where brown trout are the quarry. The Dabbler has a reputation for tempting large fish from the great loughs of Ireland. It works throughout the season. Like many big wet flies it is most effective when conditions are overcast and there is a good rolling wave.
- The standard technique is to fish the Dabbler as part of a team, lifting the rod so it dabbles enticingly in the wave. The Dabbler works either on the point or the top dropper.

TYING THE DABBLER

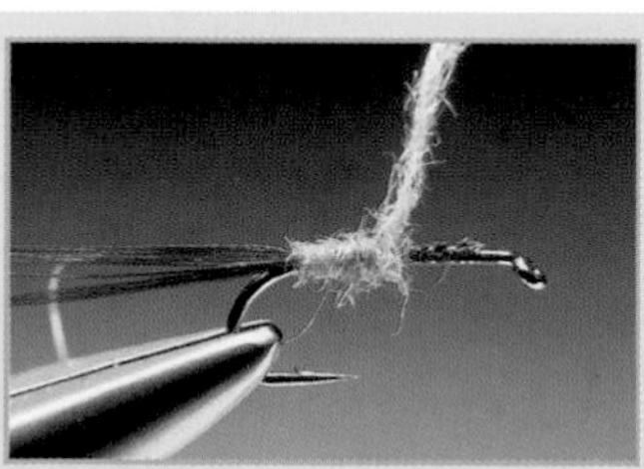

1 Wind the thread down the shank to the bend. Catch in six or eight fibres of cock pheasant tail and tinsel rib. Dub on a pinch of golden-olive seal's fur. Wind the dubbed fur along the hook in close turns.

2 Form a thick, ragged body with plenty of fibres sticking out. Leaving space for the hackles and wing, catch a long-fibred brown cock hackle in front of the body. Wind it down the body in open, evenly spaced turns.

3 Secure the hackle with the tinsel rib. Wiggle the tinsel as you wind to avoid trapping the hackle fibres. At the eye, secure tinsel and trim.

A lovely wet-fly wave on Lough Corrib

4 Take a second brown hackle slightly longer in fibre than the first. Catch it in just behind the eye and wind on three full turns to form a collar, and secure.

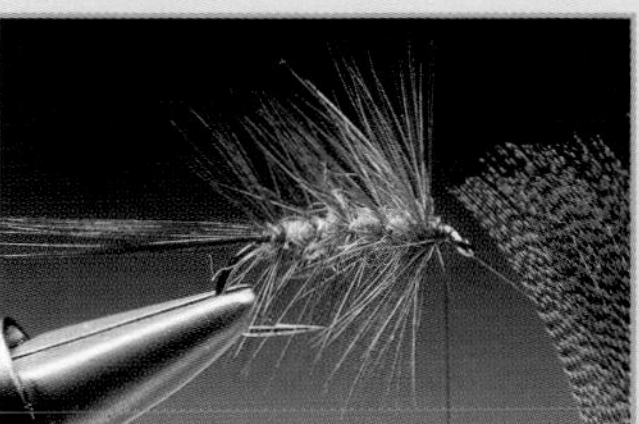

5 Remove a wide strip of bronze mallard from the feather. This should be at least three times the width of the intended wing.

6 Roll the slip of feather to form the wing before catching it in on top of the hook with tying thread. Position the wing so that it sits low over the body. Fix the wing in place with tight turns of thread, working the fibres around the sides so that they envelop the body. Trim away the waste ends of the feather before building a neat head.

Stocked Stillwater

Rainbow trout in lowland reservoirs

Some of the anglers who first fished the renowned stocked reservoirs at Chew and Blagdon in south-west England had learnt their fishing on the great wild brown trout lochs in the wilder bits of Britain. Many more hadn't. They had learnt their fishing on the coarse rivers and fisheries of lowland England. They came to fly-fishing for trout without the fetters of brown trout fly-fishing lore and ancient tradition. They were prepared to experiment, adapt and learn from anyone else who fished for these dashing rainbow trout. They learnt a lot from the Americans. Crazes in lures and flies came and went through the angling press like the crazes for hula-hoop and scoubidous through a girls' school playground.

In recent years there has been a perceptible move away from outlandish lures ripped through the depths towards the imitation of the insects, some of them tiny, that occupy the attention of trout in rich lowland reservoirs. These smaller flies are often fished very slowly, sometimes at a standstill, as befits tiny larvae and pupae. Large flies are still darted through the depths but these days they are more likely to be imitations and echoes of the meaty damselfly nymphs that can infest these waters, or the tadpoles and coarse-fish fry that haunt their margins. At the same time the fishermen who learnt their fly-fishing on the lowland reservoirs are visiting the fabled limestone loughs of Ireland and the great lochs of Scotland and bringing back ideas from these more traditional fishing communities. The world of fly-fishing has benefited immeasurably from the fruitful cross-fertilization of these two schools of stillwater fly-fishing and their flies.

Midges, Buzzers and Bloodworms

Chironomids, in their various guises, are the most important insects in lowland lakes to trout and trout fishermen alike

Those trout fortunate enough to inhabit the more productive lakes and reservoirs live in a world where their favourite food is on the menu virtually every day of the year. We're talking about chironomids, midges or buzzers: call them what you will, they are the most important food species for the stocked stillwater.

The chironomid life-cycle of interest to trout and trout fishermen begins with the bloodworm larva. This develops into the pupa – often called a buzzer (although the only buzzing is done by the adults), which migrates to the surface where it hatches into the adult midge. The insect is at its most vulnerable, and therefore of most interest to fishermen, at the pupal stage, as it travels up through the water, and during this transposition into the adult when it struggles out of its pupal skin.

The final stage is the adult, which hovers over the water in the gloaming, laying its thousands of eggs to propagate the next generation. At this time, the trout can be at their hardest to catch as they actually poke their noses out of the water to take the airborne fly half an inch from the surface film.

RELATED SUBJECT: • Using plastics p94

Larval Stage - the Bloodworm

The chironomid larva is a small worm-like creature that, depending on the species, ranges in colour from almost transparent to pale straw, olive, green and red. They also vary greatly in size, from the tiny up to almost an inch long, though the average is around half that, making a size 10–12 the ideal hook on which to tie an imitation.

The most common and conspicuous is the bright red bloodworm. The distinctive colour comes from the haemoglobin that allows it to live in an oxygen-poor black, oozy silt on a lake bed. Here the larvae lie hidden in tubes they construct using mucous to stick the silt particles together.

For much of the time they are inaccessible to the trout but they are sometimes found in open water, where they are able to swim using a lashing motion of their entire bodies. This action is difficult to imitate, though some bloodworm patterns achieve a degree of success by incorporating a long, mobile tail either of marabou or a single strand of rubber. Others rely simply on copying the colour and translucency. Either way, bloodworm imitations are most effective when fished with a very slow retrieve.

FLEXI BLOODWORM
HOOK: **Size 14 grub hook**
THREAD: **Red**
TAIL: **Dyed-red marabou**
BODY: **Red Flexifloss**

RED DIDDY
HOOK: **Size 12**
THREAD: **Red**
BODY: **Red plastic bead plus a strand of red Flexifloss doubled and twisted**

Bloodworm swim with a lashing motion of their bodies

Pupa – The 'Buzzer'

The pupa is the most vulnerable stage of the midge's life, as it must leave the protective tube in which it lived as a larva and rise to the surface so that the adult insect can emerge.

The pupa is not a strong swimmer, relying on a build-up of gas in its body to make it buoyant and help it on its journey. When the pupa reaches the surface this gas reveals itself as a silvery hue beneath the skin – which is why imitations ribbed with pearl or silver tinsel prove so effective.

The colour and size of the pupae differ in the same way as the adult chironomids. Black is the most common, and black imitations tied in a range of sizes are the ones that prove most effective overall. Trout will take all the other colours, especially olive and green, though these are more likely to be found throughout the warm summer months.

Trout feed on the pupae at all depths, and even if there is no obvious hatch it is likely that the pupae are beginning to ascend and are being picked off as they do so. When fishing chironomid pupa – 'buzzer' – imitations it is important to get their depth right. Fish deep with slim imitations on strong wire hooks – these are usually coated with varnish or epoxy resin to help them sink. For fish feeding near the surface use buzzers on light wire hooks with herl or dubbed bodies.

Fish a floating line with a long leader, sometimes in excess of 20ft, using a team of buzzers, 4–5ft apart, with the heaviest on the point. You should retrieve the line just quickly enough to keep in touch, trying to move the flies as little as possible. Many anglers seem to 'need' to move the flies. With buzzers, just leave them and wait for the line to tighten. It will if you've got it right!

The perfect conditions are a nice ripple and the boat moving at a steady pace. If you are drifting too quickly, the flies do not fish for long enough at the desired depth. At this stage you should be prepared to fish the flies on a shorter leader with a sinking line to get them down to the fish for as long as possible.

From the bank, use the same floating line set-up and simply let the buzzers drift round on the wind. Takes are easy to spot: the line slowly tightens and all you have to do is lift. 'Striking' is not usually necessary as the fish confidently swim off with the fly hooked firmly in their scissors.

Chironomid pupae come in all sorts of colours, though black is the most common

Buzzers from the stomach of a single rainbow trout from a reservoir

RELATED SUBJECT:
- Using plastics p94

OLIVE BUZZER

HOOK: Size 10–14
THREAD: Olive
BODY: Dyed-olive pheasant tail
RIB: Silver wire
THORAX: Orange seal's fur topped with olive PT fibres
WINGBUDS: Brown goose biots
BREATHERS: White Antron

FLEXI BUZZER

HOOK: Size 8–12 heavyweight grub hook
THREAD: Black
BODY: Black and red Flexifloss
THORAX: Black Flexifloss
WINGBUDS: Orange T-shirt paint
BREATHERS: White marabou

Hatching Pupa

The hatching midge pupa reaches the surface where it must break through the surface tension as the pupal skin splits and the adult fly emerges. The insect may get trapped in the surface tension or struggle to break through. Trout can target these struggles and several patterns exploit this most vulnerable stage of the midge's journey.

The Shuttlecock combines a slim abdomen with a dense plume of buoyant fibres to imitate the chironomid midge pupa as it transposes into the winged adult.

The Shuttlecock is easy to tie and, what's more important, very effective. It can be tied in a combination of sizes and colours to match those of the prevailing hatch, though the most effective colours are orange, black, fiery brown and olive.

The key to the pattern's success is the CDC wing. This keeps the fly sitting in the surface film while the slim body sinks beneath to imitate the profile of a hatching midge. The pearl tinsel rib adds that finishing touch, providing the sparkle found in the gaseous body of a fully developed midge pupa.

Don't use any floatant on this fly. The body should sink to hang enticingly below the surface.

SHUTTLECOCK

HOOK: Size 12–16 medium-weight wet-fly

THREAD: To suit body colour

WING: Natural grey CDC

RIB: Fine pearl tinsel

BODY: Seal's fur or substitute in a range of colours

TYING THE SHUTTLECOCK

1 Wind the thread a short distance down the shank to form a base for the wing. Select three fluffy, natural grey CDC feathers and place together so that their tips are level. Catch them in just behind the eye.

2 Cover the waste ends with close turns of thread. Carry the thread down to the bend and catch in 2in of fine pearl tinsel.

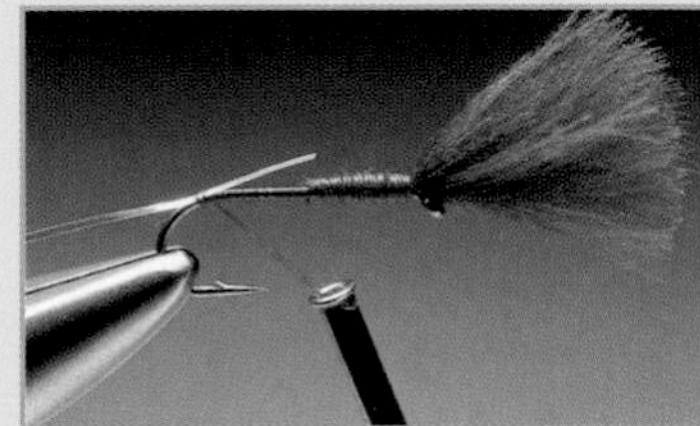

3 Dub the seal's fur on to the tying thread to form a thin rope. Starting at the bend, wind the dubbed fur along the shank in close turns until it is a short distance from the wing base. Take hold of the pearl tinsel and wind on five evenly spaced turns.

4 Secure the tinsel and trim. Take another smaller pinch of fur, dub it on to the thread and wind it to form a small thorax around the base of the wing. Take the thread underneath the wing and wind on a few turns right at the eye. Complete with a five-turn whip finish.

RELATED SUBJECTS: • Teasing out dubbing p86 • Cul-de-canard p38

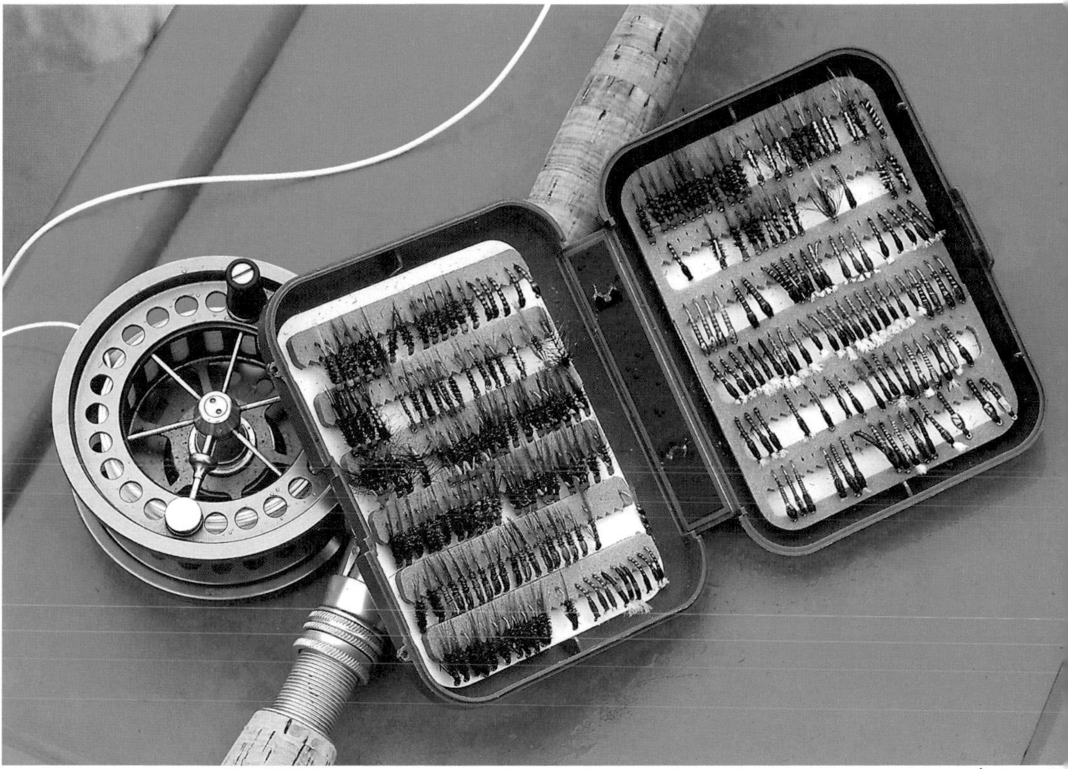

A selection of buzzer imitations

Shipman's Buzzer

This dry fly imitates the hatching midge on the surface. The original tied by Dave Shipman used white Antron fibres at head and tail to float the fly. CDC fibres float even better than Antron. The method of tying is almost the same as for the Shuttlecock Buzzer but a second bunch of CDC fibres is tied in at the tail before the ribbing material.

Shipman's Buzzer is fished dry. Its floatation is improved if the fibres of fur dubbing are teased out from the finished body with a piece of Velcro. Floatant is applied to the body but be careful not to get any oil on the CDC fibres.

tip

- Both these hatching midge imitations are most effective in the summer months when the natural insects are hatching and the trout are feeding close to the surface.

Adult Midges

Trout will take the adult midge most often at two particular points during its life-cycle.

The first is when the midge bursts free of its pupal skin, while positioned right in the water's surface film. At this stage the chironomid is extremely vulnerable as it takes a few precious seconds before the adult is ready to take flight and trout will cruise along sipping them in, often while the insect is still partially trapped in its shuck.

Another major opportunity for the fish is when the chironomid returns to the water to lay its eggs. Especially on calm summer evenings, females can be seen skimming along the water's surface, their abdomens curved as they hold a small parcel of eggs at their tips. Occasionally you will come across the 'balling buzzer' phenomenon, where females are swarmed by literally dozens of males intent on mating, creating a mass, or ball, of tiny flying insects.

tip

- Tease out dubbed fly bodies to make the fly more 'buzzy'. This can be done with a dubbing needle but it is safer and more effective to use the 'hook' side of a piece of Velcro.

Preparing to fish, early morning

RELATED SUBJECT: • Dyeing feathers p66

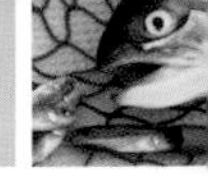

Claret Hopper

Although called a Hopper, visually this pattern has more in common with a small daddy-long-legs than a grasshopper. Actually, it was tied to represent neither and instead is very effective during a hatch of midge. It is also a great general dry fly, working well throughout the season, even when there is little obvious surface activity.

This claret version is one of the most effective colours but it also works well when tied in black, red, orange or fiery brown. Whatever the colour, all Hoppers have the same trailing legs tied from strands of cock pheasant tail – each knotted once. These legs provide the Hopper's distinct silhouette and also work in the water's surface.

Even though it is intended to float, the pattern should not be tied on a light-wire hook. Not only is this tempting fate, if a big fish is hooked, but the hook needs to be quite heavy so that the finished fly sits low in the surface. The hackle fibres can be clipped underneath the hook to help this.

Like other stillwater dry-flies the body is made of dubbed fur, which is normally teased out before being fished to accentuate the translucency and sparkle of the material. Further sparkle is added by the use of pearl tinsel as a rib.

CLARET HOPPER

HOOK: Size 10–12

THREAD: Black

RIB: Pearl tinsel

BODY: Claret seal's fur

LEGS: Knotted strands of cock pheasant tail

HACKLE: Brown cock hackle

Bob's Bits

Bob's Bits is a classic example of a dry fly designed specifically for stillwater trout fishing.

Unlike traditional dry flies, which rely on stiff cock hackle fibres to keep them afloat, this pattern uses a much sparser hackle and teased-out body material so that it sits right in the surface film rather than on it.

The body consists of a pinch of seal's fur or substitute dubbed thinly on to the tying thread. The resulting effect should be slim but well teased out so that the fibres catch the light and also, when treated with floatant, help to grab the water's surface. Red, black, olive and brown are the most effective colours. Use it when adult midges can be seen hatching off in numbers.

BOB'S BITS

HOOK: Size 10–14

THREAD: Brown

RIB: Fine silver wire

BODY: Red seal's fur

WING: White hackle fibres

HACKLE: Brown cock hackle

Flighty Damsels

Damselflies – or their nymphs – are a meaty mouthful in lowland lakes

Damselflies are a familiar sight on the margins of most lowland lakes and slow-flowing rivers in the long days of summer. They are closely related to dragonflies but the damselfly is slimmer, more delicate and fluttering, and holds its wings together when resting.

The nymph is large and meaty and forms an important part of the lake trout's diet. The adults range in colour from red to green and blue – the latter being the most common. The males are more brightly coloured than the females, which are usually pale green or brown, depending upon the species.

Although trout will take the adults, slashing through the surface in the attempt, damselflies are preyed upon most heavily as nymphs. The aquatic nymph is just over an inch long when fully grown, with a slim abdomen tipped by three leaf-like gills. It spends most of its time preying on smaller invertebrates, concealed in weed and well camouflaged by its green coloration.

It is not a perfect disguise because trout feed on the immature nymphs

DAMSELFLY NYMPH

HOOK: Size 10–12 wet-fly

THREAD: Olive

TAIL: Olive marabou

RIB: Fine gold wire

BODY: Olive marabou

THORAX: Olive fur

HACKLE: Dyed-olive partridge

THORAX COVER: Dyed-olive pheasant tail

EYES: Small pearl glass beads

A scenic view of Eyebrook reservoir

RELATED SUBJECT:

• Dyeing feathers p66

even quite early in the year, well before the insect's main emergence time, from late May through June and into July, when the nymphs break cover in order to transpose into winged adults. During this period large numbers of nymphs swim along, just under the surface, by lashing their abdomens from side to side with a very distinctive action. The most effective damselfly nymph imitations incorporate a long mobile tail, of marabou or hair, to imitate this movement.

There are many damselfly imitations. This one has glass bead eyes which add an up-and-down motion as it is retrieved.

fishing the damsel

- Damselflies are most numerous on rich lowland waters. The size of water doesn't matter so long as there are extensive weed beds and shallows, which provide an ideal habitat for the naturals.
- Imitation damselfly nymphs should be fished singly or as the point-fly of a team of nymphs. Floating or intermediate lines are the most effective, the fly being fished around the edges of weed beds with a steady figure-of-eight retrieve.

TYING THE DAMSEL NYMPH

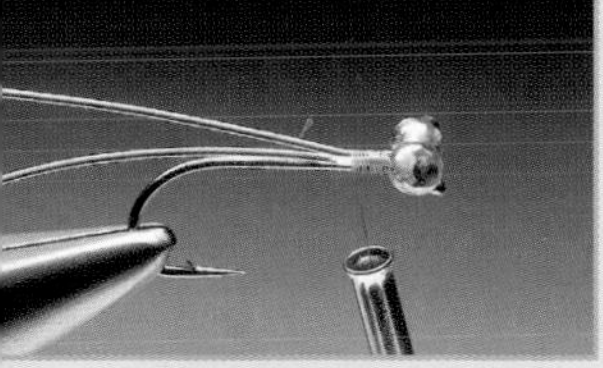

1 Form two eyes by fixing small glass beads on to strands of 20lb nylon, which have been melted at one end. Position the beads on top of the hook and fix in place with tight turns of olive thread.

2 Remove the excess nylon and carry the tying thread down the shank in close turns. Catch a small pinch of fluffy marabou fibres in at the bend to form the tail. Then catch in, at its base, 3in of the fine gold wire.

3 Take a second pinch of less fluffy marabou fibres taken from close to the plume-tip. Catch them in by their points at the base of the tail. Carry the thread back up the shank. Take hold of the marabou and, allowing the fibres to spread flat, wind it up to the tying thread.

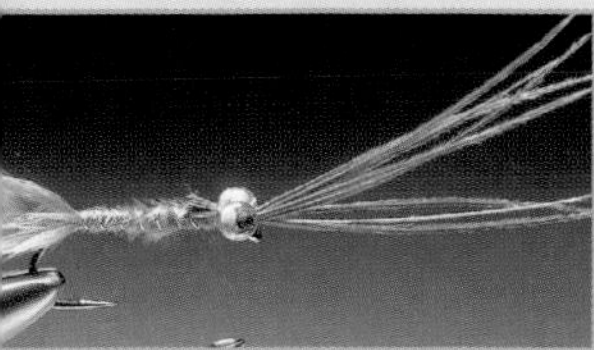

4 Secure the loose ends of the marabou and trim. Wind the gold wire over the body in evenly spaced turns wound in the opposite spiral to the marabou. Trim excess wire. Catch in a bunch of dyed-olive pheasant tail fibres between the bead eyes. Allow the tips to project over the hook eye.

5 Catch a dyed-olive partridge hackle, by its tip, behind the bead eyes. Wind on two or three turns of the partridge feather.

6 Secure the hackle with thread and remove the excess. Dub on a pinch of olive fur and wind two turns down the shank to form the thorax. Stroke the hackle fibres down then pull the pheasant tail fibres over the back of the thorax. Secure with thread before casting off with a whip finish. Finally, trim the pheasant tail fibres to suggest wing buds.

Diawl Bach

The deadly 'little devil' that rules the reservoirs

The Diawl Bach nymph is regarded as one of the deadliest nymphs for all stillwaters. It was originally fished as point-fly on a floating line in partnership with a couple of Buzzers. The simple set-up worked well and its fame spread. Around the world the Diawl Bach is now regarded as the nymph to rely on in stillwaters. Competitive boat-fishers wouldn't go afloat without the original pattern and its descendants.

The Diawl Bach is a suggestive pattern. It looks like nothing in particular but suggests a bit of everything, and probably a bit extra, to a feeding trout. The Diawl Bach nymph works well when buzzers are hatching, when sedges are hatching and even when nothing is hatching. The pattern also works when pin-fry are around, corixa feeders take it, and even snail-feeders find it irresistible. What more can one ask of a fly?

Such is its pulling power that during a buzzer hatch, a trout will often grab the Diawl Bach rather

STANDARD DIAWL BACH

HOOK: **Size 10**

BODY: **Bronze peacock herl**

RIB: **Fine copper wire**

TAIL AND THROAT HACKLE: **Red cock hackle fibres**

A Blagdon brownie that fell to a Diawl Bach fished 'static'

RELATED SUBJECT: • Jungle-cock cheeks p117

than the 'proper' chironomid imitation. As a result, competition anglers often replace the Buzzers with smaller Diawl Bachs. A three-fly cast for the evening rise consists of a size 12 longshank Diawl Bach on the point, a size 10 on the middle dropper and a size 12 on the bob. This particular partnership works beautifully.

From bank or boat, fishing the Diawl Bach should normally be a gentle affair. With the retrieve something between a crawl and a dead stop, it is known as the 'static nymph' technique. 'Static', however, isn't quite the right word as the flies are more likely to be taken as they fall through the water than during the retrieve itself, even a very slow retrieve.

Watching for takes – rather than waiting for a pull – can mean the difference between success and failure. The method is simplicity itself. Using a floating line, simply hold the rod tip about a foot above the water and watch the length of line that hangs between the rod tip and the water. When you make the retrieve, the line will straighten and then fall as you pause. When a fish picks up the fly, the line will either stay taut when it should have gone slack, or else it will appear to 'flick' straight as if someone had taken hold of it and given it a good tug.

Whatever the signal, it is impossible to miss, and the response must be a solid strike – just as if you were hitting a trout rising to a dry fly. If you fail to strike quickly enough, the fish will often drop the fly and there is nothing felt at the hand. If you continue with the retrieve, the fish will often come back and have another go if it has felt no resistance. In effect, this presents you with a second and on some ocassions even a third opportunity to catch a trout on one cast.

The remarkable thing about the method is that if you were not watching the line – and most anglers don't – you would be blissfully unaware that a trout had actually seen the fly, never mind taken it in its mouth.

Here is a variety of 'little devils', just three of the dozens of variations to be found in the reservoir

JUNGLE COCK DIAWL BACH
HOOK: Size 10
BODY: Bronze peacock herl
RIB: Fine silver wire
TAIL AND THROAT HACKLE: Red cock hackle fibres
CHEEKS: Jungle cock

GOLD-RIBBED DIAWL BACH
HOOK: Size 12
BODY: Bronze peacock herl
RIB: Medium gold holographic tinsel
TAIL AND THROAT HACKLE: Red cock hackle fibres

SILVER-HEADED DIAWL BACH
HOOK: Size 10
BODY: Bronze peacock herl
RIB: Fine silver wire
TAIL AND THROAT HACKLE: Red cock hackle fibres
THORAX: Silver holographic tinsel

Cold Starts

Rainbow trout can be fished through the coldest months of the year

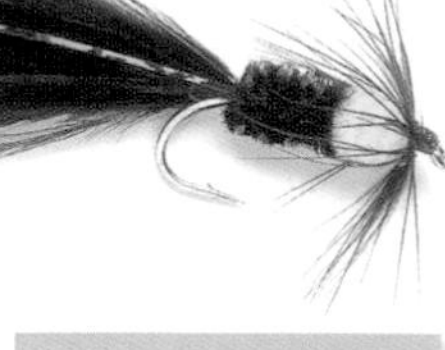

Black and lime green is a very effective colour combination for stillwater trout flies, especially when used early and late in the season. Several large flies with larger reputations have featured a black body with a bright lime green or yellow 'aiming point'. The Viva and Montana have been early season reservoir favourites with anglers for many years.

The Green Pea uses this high-contrast combination and combines it with a highly mobile tail of black marabou to trigger a response when water temperatures are low and the trout reluctant to feed – a time

GREEN PEA

HOOK: Size 10–12 wet-fly

THREAD: Black

WEIGHT: Fine lead wire

TAIL: Black marabou with two or three strands of pearl tinsel (optional)

BODY: Black chenille

THORAX: Fluorescent lime-green chenille

HACKLE: Black cock hackle

TYING THE GREEN PEA

1 Wind fine lead wire in close turns to cover about two-thirds of the shank. Leave a gap to the rear of the underbody for the tail. Secure in place with tying thread (add a drop of superglue first if necessary). Remove a long, slim tuft of black marabou from the plume.

2 Catch in the marabou opposite the barb to form a long tail. Secure with tight thread wraps over the waste ends. Catch in two or three fine strands of pearl tinsel or Flashabou of the same length as the marabou.

3 Take 3in of black chenille. Remove the fibre to expose the core at one end. Catch in the core at the base of the tail. Take the thread two-thirds of the way along the shank. Wind the chenille in close turns.

RELATED SUBJECT: • Weighting flies p24

change of colour

- To save the bother of changing threads when tying a fly that calls for different coloured threads for body and head, complete the fly and run a permanent marker pen along the last two inches of the body thread before forming the head.

when more imitative patterns are often ignored.

When using marabou the aim is to impart as much movement as possible to the finished fly. It is a good idea to keep the tail long and the body short rather than vice versa. Often a size 10, or even 12, standard wet-fly model is used, the tail being two or three times the length of the hook. This way there is enough of the soft feather tail to give a wonderfully attractive action with a steady figure-of-eight retrieve.

A little weight in the form of lead wire is used in the underbody, not to make the fly sink very quickly but simply to counteract the drag of the long marabou tail. Don't overdo the weight: the beguiling sinuous action of the tail needs a slow retrieve. If the fly is too heavy it will end up snagging the bottom.

Anglers have found the Green Pea fly to be a deadly pattern used on the whole range of stocked waters. It can be used to catch fish throughout the season but it is at its most effective early and late in the season when the trout are active but their natural food is not abundant.

MONTANA
HOOK: Size 8–10 longshank
THREAD: Black
TAIL: Black cock hackles
BODY: Black chenille
THORAX: Lime-green chenille
THORAX COVER: Black chenille
HACKLE: Black cock hackle palmered through the thorax

4 Secure the chenille and trim. Take 2in of fluorescent lime-green chenille, expose the core and catch it in at the front of the black section. Wind this, too, in close turns to form a short, bright, aiming point. Two or three turns is enough on a hook of this size. Secure and trim.

5 Catch in a black cock hackle immediately in front of the fluorescent green chenille. Wind on two or three full turns. Secure the hackle and trim. Stroke the fibres back over the body before building a small, neat head.

tip

- When using marabou, pinch off the ends of the fibres rather than cutting them level. This way a softer, more natural-looking effect is created.

Plastic Surgery

Plastics have got a lot going for them – as long as you don't overdo it

They're tough, easy to use and don't deteriorate for a very long time. Modern plastics are extremely useful for fly-tying, but always make sure to use them in combination with at least one other more mobile product such as fur or feather. There's a temptation to make a perfect facsimile of an insect and plastics can certainly look great, but they lack that bit of 'life', so essential if the fly is to be effective. It's all too easy to get carried away and forget that you are tying a fly to catch fish.

The list of plastics used in tying flies is simply vast. The variety is now so great that the problem is not in finding them, but in choosing the right one to do the job.

STRIPS

Plastic strip comes in varying degrees of stretchability. Its main uses are either wound as a body, or simply laid over the fly to create a shellback or a thorax cover. Some makes have the same texture either side while others have a dull and a shiny side. The latter is more useful. Most strips come in a small range of colours: yellow, grey, tan, brown, various shades of olive, and clear.

PLASTIC SHEETS

These are often the same stuff as the plastic strip but in sheets. They are used in the same way but you have to cut them to the correct width first. Most sheets, like the strips, are sold in plain colours, but a few are available with a mottled effect, making them great for tying imitations of caseless caddis larvae.

NYLON MONOFILAMENT

Very fine, clear monofil is brilliant for ribbing small, delicate-bodied flies. The nylon itself is very tough but, being clear, doesn't affect the overall look of the fly as a wire rib would. What's more, being very light, it adds a negligible amount of weight – especially important when tying small dry-flies. Monofilament nylon can also be used to protect delicate materials, such as peacock herl, where the pattern doesn't actually call for a rib.

TUBING

Fine, plastic tubing sold under brand names such as Ultra Lace and Larva Lace is great for tying both bodies and ribs. The colour range is large and there are enough shades to tie a wide range of effective nymph and pupa imitations. As these products both stretch and wind flat, they can produce a very slim effect – perfect, in fact, for midge pupae imitations. If you are really clever you can even thread a strand of pearl lurex through the centre of the tube to add an inner sparkle.

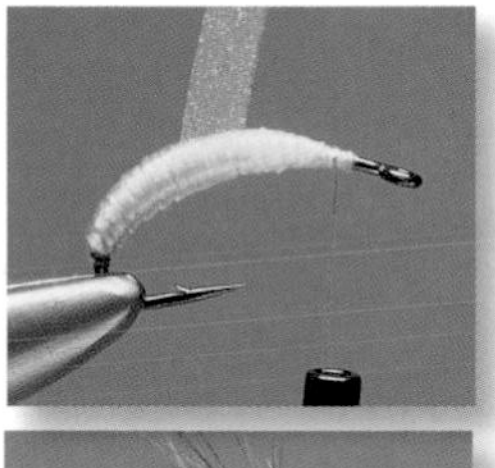

STRANDS

There are many types and makes of plastic strands on the market. The most popular are the thin, very elastic types known by names such as Flexifloss, Spanflex and Stretch Floss. These can be used as single colours or mixed together either to form an entire body and thorax or simply as a ribbing material. The thinnest diameter strands have a great deal of flexibility and can also be used in place of rubber legs to give large nymphs and lures an added 'kick'.

The more solid, less stretchable, varieties are really only useful as a ribbing material. Vinyl products, such as Magic Glass and Swannundaze, can be used to form a tough rib or, by applying close turns, an entire translucent body.

PLASTIC RAFFIA

Also known as Raffene, this is the artificial version of raffia which has been used in fly-tying for many years. The plastic version is far better than the original as it is much more translucent and doesn't deteriorate. It also comes in a far wider rage of colours. When using plastic raffia, always wet it first. Otherwise, when it is immersed in water, it will stretch and become very loose.

POLYTHENE

Clear polythene was probably the first plastic to be used in fly-tying. It can form a shell-back on shrimp imitations or can be stretched and wound along the shank to create interesting translucent bodies. It is great for tying small fry imitations such as the Polystickle and Sinfoil's Fry. When using polythene, always cut the strip twice as wide as you need then gently stretch it before tying in. This process not only makes the polythene even more transparent, but helps it to wind more easily.

Fry-Fishing

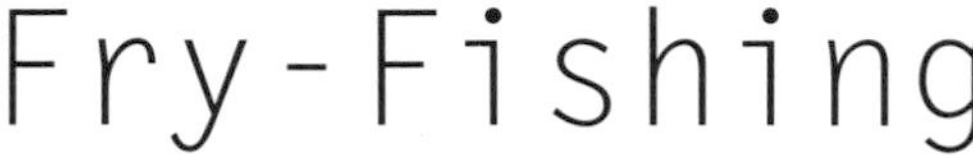

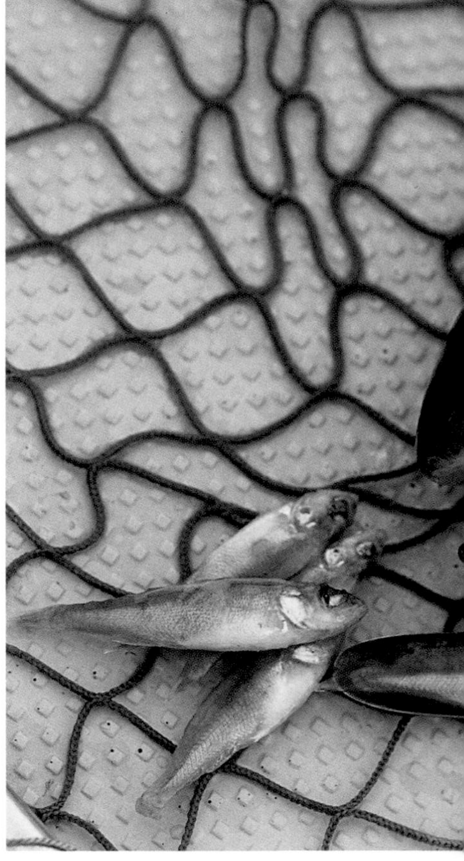

The biggest trout come to gorge on the autumn shoals of coarse-fish fry

You will see a scattering of silver rain, like a handful of confetti thrown into the margins of the lake. Trout are charging through the shoals of fry that hide amongst the weeds and shallows. They will return to pick up the dead and dying or cruise the margins, picking up any hapless individual separated from the shoal.

Lures based on the highly mobile rabbit and mink furs are great catchers of trout feeding on fry, but they do have a drawback. Being very dense, the fur holds the water, making it heavy and difficult to cast, especially if the lure is a big one. EP Fibre, a wonderfully translucent material named after its inventor, American fly-dresser Enrico Puglisi, weighs almost nothing and sheds water the moment it is lifted out.

A single fly attached to a 15ft leader of 10–12lb nylon and fished on a floating line will cover most bank-fishing situations. Once the lure has settled in the water, give it a couple of short pulls to alert any fish in the vicinity and then retrieve it with a slow to medium-fast figure-of-eight movement, punctuated with a few short pulls to help convince a following trout that its lunch is about to disappear.

EP FRY

HOOK: Size 4–6 shortshank carp hook

THREAD: White

BODY AND WING: EP Fibre, white and dark grey for roach, dark olive for perch. Both have a few strands of silver Flashabou tinsel or similar. Colour the perch imitation with orange and black waterproof markers

EYES: Stick-on eyes or sequins coloured with a waterproof marker. Varnish the eyes and head with epoxy varnish

RELATED SUBJECT:

• Spinning deer hair p104

From the boat, switch to a sinking line fishing in depths of up to 12ft around the weedbeds.

Floating Fry

There are times, when they are feeding on dead and dying coarse-fish fry, when trout will take a floating imitation and no other. Various materials such as foam have been used to fashion effective floating fry but the original and still the best is deer hair. It is soft and buoyant but will also absorb a little water, with a gentle squeeze. This allows the fly to be fished barely floating, which is just how the real thing sits, with hardly any part showing above the surface. The result is a 'fly' that will fool even big, grown-on trout, which is just as well, since creating floating fry from deer hair is rather time-consuming. However, if those big, back end fish are the target, it is well worth the effort.

Deer hair can be used to fashion most prey species but the two most common are perch and roach. Both have basically the same shape, so the main decision when beginning to tie is whether the pattern is to be tied upright or flat so that it floats on its side. The latter method is the most natural position for a dead fish.

FLOATING FRY

HOOK: Size 6–12 longshank

THREAD: White 6/0 or stronger

TAIL: Grey or orange marabou and strands of pearl Flashabou

BODY: White deer hair coloured with waterproof markers

FINS: Pearl Flashabou

EYES: Stick-on decals

tips

- Late summer and autumn are the times when trout most regularly feed on coarse-fish fry.
- A floating line is used with this pattern. As the Floating Fry is both large and air-resistant, a weight-forward line rated 8–9 is needed to cast it. A strong leader of at least 8lb breaking strain is also needed to prevent breaking the fly off while casting.
- Don't pack the deer hair overly tight when creating the body of the Floating Fry. Aim to create a soft body which will float but will still absorb a little water when being fished.

Rattling with Snails

Gourmet trout can gorge on escargots

Freshwater snails vary considerably in both size and shape but the vast majority that end up inside the stomach of a trout range from a quarter to half-an-inch in length, with an oval shell coming to a slight point at the rear. The colour varies from black through to olive: shades of olive are by far the most common.

Snails are plentiful in loch margins during high summer

Though trout will feed on snails throughout the season, high summer is when snail numbers boom and other forms of life tend to wane.

Most snails are taken nearer the bottom as they graze algae from stones and weed fronds with a tooth-covered tongue known as a radula. This is normally in relatively shallow water, up to about six feet in depth, where the light penetration is great enough for the algae to grow and support the greatest concentrations of snails.

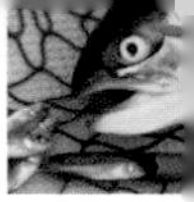

There are times when trout feed so heavily on snails that they positively rattle when caught. Snail-feeding trout are seemingly oblivious to the hard shells. They simply swallow the snails whole and let the digestive juices in their stomachs dissolve the soft tissues within. Feeding on snails can't be that comfortable as the fish's vent can become quite distended from passing the undigested, but now empty shells.

While the majority of snails are picked off on the bottom, there is another way in which trout take the naturals. Sometimes large numbers of snails rise to the surface and drift along in the currents. The phenomenon can occur at any time in the summer and has been linked to de-oxygenation of the water. When the trout take snails off the surface, the rise form is reminiscent of that of a hatching midge – but all midge imitations are ignored.

Catching snail-feeding trout on purpose-designed imitations can be difficult. Patterns that have been used with success include the Black and Peacock Spider, the Chenille Snail in olive or black and the Deer Hair Snail. Perversely, an olive nymph or a small damselfly nymph imitation is often as effective as anything.

BLACK & PEACOCK SPIDER

HOOK: Size 8–12

THREAD: Black

BODY: Peacock herl

HACKLE: Black hen

added strength

- To strengthen a fly using peacock herl, twist either the tying thread or a length of fine copper wire and the herl into a rope before forming the body.

CHENILLE SNAIL

HOOK: Size 8–12

THREAD: To match body

BODY: Olive or black chenille

HACKLE: Olive or black hen

DEER HAIR SNAIL

HOOK: Size 8–12

THREAD: Brown

BODY: Spun natural deer hair, clipped to shape

Sea Trout

& Salmon

Fly-fishing for salmon and trout is an enigma. Salmon do not eat in fresh water so why do they take a fly? From the fisherman's point of view, of course, it doesn't matter why salmon take a fly: it only matters that they do. We presume that brown trout take a fly as something to eat and that gives us a rationale for creating patterns and choosing which pattern to use and when. Many very successful trout flies look nothing like anything the trout would ever eat – but they still work. And so it is with salmon flies. They work.

Some patterns undoubtedly work better than others. These become popular. Thoughtful anglers, on the quest for the irresistible fly, try to analyze the secret of their success and come up with new combinations of colour, form and movement.

The key to success for a salmon pattern fly is that it inspires confidence in the angler. A confident angler fishes better knowing he has the right thing on the end. This increases his chances of success and the reputation of the pattern grows, more fishermen use it, and so it catches more fish – and so on.

This importance of reputation and performance, combined with continual experimentation and tinkering, accounts for the dominance of a small number of universally accepted patterns among an infinite and bewildering array of variants. The patterns covered in this section concentrate on the giants of the genre.

Sea trout

Sea trout in a loch are often taken on flies that imitate natural insects. The Bibio, Daddy-long-legs and Black Gnat seem to be equally effective for sea trout and the native browns. This has led to a supposition that returning sea trout feed as actively as the resident browns.

Scientific evidence, together with the observations of authorities such as Kingsmill Moore and Hugh Falkus, strongly suggest that adult sea trout behave like adult salmon in adopting a non-feeding habit on their return to freshwater. Stomach analysis of both species may reveal the occasional item, but this is not evidence of active feeding as such, and it is just as likely to be the odd cigarette end or a twig as it is an insect or crustacean.

Things are further complicated by the fact that a proportion of smaller sea trout, up to 1lb, may enter the river and then return to the sea at various times during the season with no intention of spawning until the next year. These fish may carry on feeding actively on anything available and are probably the reason why the confusion arises.

The best approach is to assume that most sea trout, particularly the larger ones, take a lure or fly for reasons of interest, curiosity, annoyance or aggression rather than the need to provide sustenance, and so select your pattern accordingly. Local patterns and custom are usually a good guide.

Classic Sea Trout

Classic sea trout fishing begins in the darkness of a short summer night when these shy fish leave their resting places in the depths of the pools to move higher up the river

tip

- When fishing for sea trout on a moonlit night, use a fly with a silver body to reflect the light. A fly with a darker, thicker body that throws a bigger silhouette is more effective on a very dark night.

The Medicine

The late Hugh Falkus, the undisputed guru for a generation of sea trout fishermen, was the master of river night-fishing. His favourite, all-round sea trout pattern was the Medicine.

The Medicine is a simple, lightly dressed fly, reminiscent of the small fish that provide much of the sea-trout's diet when in saltwater.

In the original Medicine, silver paint was used for the body to keep it as slim as possible. Today most are tied with flat silver tinsel, which is less troublesome as there's no need to wait for it to dry.

A slim low-water single is the preferred hook as it lacks bulk and also holds fish well. Large hooks, sizes 2–6, are usual, but an 8 works well in low water. Although revered as a first-class sea-trout fly, the Medicine is also very useful during a run of grilse.

THE MEDICINE

HOOK: Size 2–8 low-water salmon single

THREAD: Red

BODY: Flat silver tinsel

RIB: Silver wire

HACKLE: Dyed-blue cock hackle

WING: Speckled grey mallard

The Allrounder

This Welsh pattern has gained a reputation as an exceptionally effective sea-trout fly. The Allrounder combines elements from several earlier sea-trout flies. It has the iridescent green peacock sword and red wing of the Alexandra with a basic black hairwing to produce a pattern that really does live up to its name. The seal's fur body and the three-stage wing produce a very dense silhouette ideal for night-fishing. Not surprisingly, it also boasts cheeks of jungle cock, which many consider an absolute must for sea trout after dark. It might seem a little over the top after the simplicity of slim patterns like the Medicine but the two styles complement each other on a cast.

This is the standard tying of the Allrounder but many regions have their own little twist on the pattern. A favourite on the River Taf omits the red section of the wing, while a version from the Tawe valley uses tippets rather than golden pheasant topping for the tail. It may be tied as a tube fly for searching out deep pools, but it is generally dressed on size 6–10 wet-fly hooks. It is the overall density that makes it so effective and the thickness of the body and wing are altered to suit local tastes.

ALLROUNDER

HOOK: Size 6–10 wet-fly

THREAD: Black

TAIL: Golden pheasant topping

BODY: Black seal's fur

RIB: Oval silver tinsel

HACKLE: Black cock hackle

WING: Black squirrel tail under red squirrel tail

TOPPING: Strands of green peacock sword

CHEEKS: Jungle cock

The Wake Lure

The classic way to bring sea trout to the surface

The original surface lures made popular by Hugh Falkus were constructed, rather than tied, from buoyant materials such as cork or goose quill. While these patterns will still catch fish, there are more modern materials available which are also lighter, softer and more yielding, and which have a definite advantage over the old ones.

This version of the Wake Lure is tied with a combination of deer hair and foam so that it is not only buoyant but also relatively soft. The result is a fly that is easier to cast and is taken more confidently, which results in fewer missed takes where the fish merely feels the hard body of the fly and rejects it before it is hooked.

WAKE LURE

HOOK: **Size 2–4 longshank;** *(on flyer):* **10–12 treble attached to 20lb nylon**

THREAD: **Brown 8/0;** *(on flyer):* **Black 8/0**

TAIL: **Gold Crystal Hair**

BODY: **Grey deer hair;** *(on flyer):* **Flat gold tinsel and gold wire**

HEAD: **White foam**

TYING THE WAKE LURE

1 Fix a treble in the vice and run the thread on at the eye. Loop 6in of 20lb nylon around the back of the hook and feed the ends through the eye. Wind thread over the nylon.

2 Catch in two inches of gold wire at the bend, then take the thread back to the eye. Now catch in the flat gold tinsel near the eye and wind it in touching turns along the shank of the treble.

3 Wind the tinsel back to the eye. Secure and trim. Rib the body in even turns with the gold wire. Secure it at the eye, remove the excess and cast off with a whip finish.

7 Take a large bunch of grey deer hair and position it at the hook bend with two or three loose turns of the tying thread.

8 Add some further turns of thread and pull tight. This will cause the hair to flare and spin around the hook to form a dense ruff.

9 Draw the hair back and secure it with thread turns wound directly in front. Add further bunches of hair and repeat until most of the shank has been covered.

RELATED SUBJECT:

• Flying trebles p108

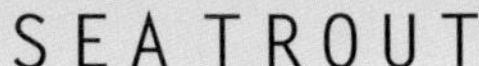

fishing the wake lure

- The Wake Lure is a pattern for an inky black night when it should be swung across pools and deeper runs where there is enough current to help the fly to drag. Use a floating line and a strong leader. The Wake Lure must be kept moving across the surface: if its wake stops for any reason, a following fish will turn away. When the fish does take, never strike – simply let the line tighten before lifting the rod.

Even so, most Wake Lures have the addition of a small flying treble projecting from the bend of the main hook – just to be on the safe side. On a dark muggy night sea trout can show a real liking for a fly that makes a big disturbance on the water's surface. In the right conditions, this style of fishing is extremely exciting and will often produce a big fish when other methods are proving ineffective.

Though it would seem that colour has little relevance in the dead of night, this pattern is tied in two versions. One has a body of black deer hair and a head of black foam, while the one shown here uses plain, grey hair and white foam.

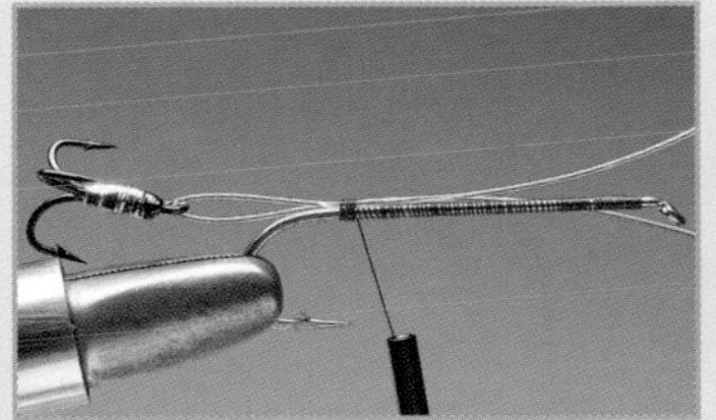

4 Now fix the longshank hook in the vice and run the brown thread from eye to bend. At the bend, catch in the two strands of nylon from the treble. Make sure the treble sits in line with the hook.

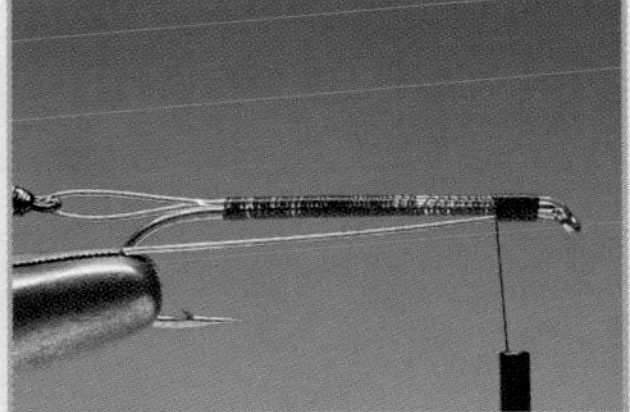

5 Secure the ends of the nylon to the entire shank using the thread. Trim one strand but pass the other through the eye and fold it back along the shank. Secure with more turns of thread.

6 Coat shank of both hook and treble with clear varnish or epoxy resin. Leave to dry. Wind on strong tying thread. Tie in a bunch of gold Crystal Hair to form a tail long enough to reach the treble hook.

10 Cast off the tying thread at the eye with a whip finish. With scissors, trim the hair to shape. Trim the underside of the hook more than the top so that the point is not masked.

11 Pierce a small square of white foam with a needle. Smear some clear epoxy glue to the front of the deer-hair body and the bare hook shank. Push the foam over the eye of the hook so that it sits tightly against the body.

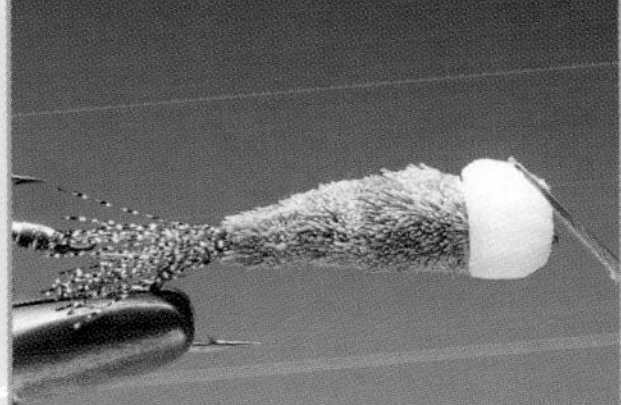

12 When the glue has set, trim the foam to shape with scissors. Trim the foam slowly and carefully to form the finished head.

Sea Trout in the Sun

Dream the impossible dream

Although by far the best chance of success is between dusk and dawn, sea trout can also be caught successfully in daylight.

The cream of daytime sea-trouting comes when the river is clearing after a small summer flood. Then an unobtrusive 5lb leader should deliver something like a Red Twist.

The Red Twist is one of a series of patterns carrying the same name which were developed for catching sea trout in daylight. The name simply refers to the turns or twists of hackle.

All the Twists are tied on fine, outpoint trebles to maximize the hooking potential of the fly, and all

TYING THE RED TWIST

1 Run the tying thread down the shank and catch in 2in of red floss. Cover the waste end of floss with turns of thread and wind on a few turns of the floss to form a short tag. Catch in the fine silver wire rib in front of the tag.

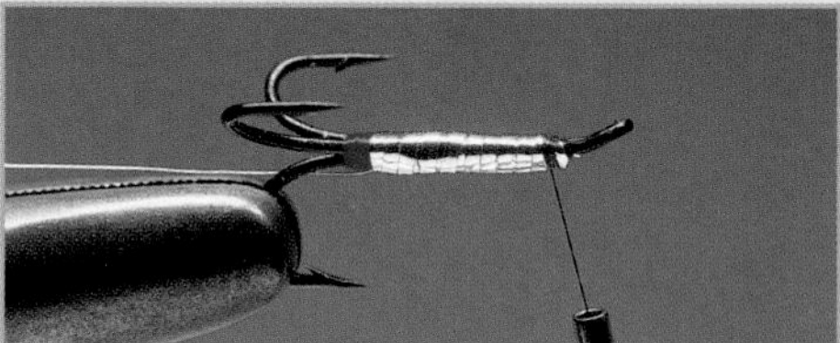

2 Cover the waste ends with close turns of thread to create an even base for the body. Catch in 3in of flat silver tinsel near the eye. Wind the tinsel in close turns down to the tag. Take care not to snag the tinsel on the hook points. Wind the tinsel back over itself in close turns to form a double layer.

3 Wind the silver wire rib over the body in evenly spaced turns. Secure the loose end and trim. Catch in a long-fibred dyed-red cock hackle at the eye. Wind on two or three turns to form the first section of the collar. Secure.

4 Catch in a dyed-black cock hackle with fibres slightly longer than those of the red. Wind on two or three turns. Secure the waste end and trim. Stroke the hackle fibres back over the body and position them with thread turns. Build a small head and make a whip finish.

RED TWIST

HOOK: Size 8–14 longshank treble

THREAD: Black

TAG: Red fluorescent floss

BODY: Flat silver tinsel

RIB: Silver wire

INNER HACKLE: Dyed-red cock hackle

OUTER HACKLE: Dyed-black cock hackle

have silver bodies and black outer hackles. They are varied by changing the colour of the inner hackle. This can be yellow, orange, green or blue though it is the red version that has become the most popular. The red colour combination gives it more than a passing resemblance to a Butcher, a favourite old fly once used for catching sea trout.

The hackles are usually wound separately to provide two distinct colour bands but, for variety, they may also be wound together to produce an effect like that of the Bumble series (see pages 72–3). The length of the hackles is also varied so that they sit at different angles to the body, creating either a more streamlined fly or a bushier one.

Cock hackles are used in preference to hen hackles as they are stiffer and create more fish-attracting disturbance in the water.

Thompson's Terror

What a splendid, confidence-inspiring name for another fly with a solid reputation for taking sea trout during the day. It was invented by Bob Thompson, a water bailiff on the Border Esk – where they know a thing or two about sea trout. It bears a resemblance to the family Twist but its original model was the Greenwell's Spider, a pattern long regarded as a useful fly when attempting to interest sea trout by day on this notoriously difficult water. Since those days it has changed its body to silver and sometimes sports a yellow tail.

Thompson's Terror is traditionally dressed on a double hook, which keeps it on an even keel in the current.

THOMPSON'S TERROR

HOOK: Size 10–14 double

THREAD: Pale primrose

TAIL *(optional)*: Fluorescent yellow floss

BODY: Flat silver tinsel criss-crossed with the tying thread to leave the tinsel glinting through

HACKLE: Greenwell saddle hackle with a shiny, greenish centre. Saddle hackles are not as stiff as those from a cock cape, making the fly more mobile

Sea Trout in Loch, Llyn and Lough

There are lakes to be found where the boat fisherman can cast across the waves uncertain whether he is fishing for salmon, sea trout or brown trout. It is not surprising then that the sea trout flies that have gained their fish-taking credentials on such waters bear a close resemblance to the flies used on all the great natural lakes of the north and west.

Morning Glory

From somewhere over the rainbow

There comes the day when, for no obvious reason, the sea trout make fools of us all by rejecting flies blended from subtle muted tones and embrace only a garish creation that was originally tied to appeal to the most gullible rainbow trout. That is the day for the Morning Glory.

Flies don't come much brighter than this descendant of the traditional Kingfisher Butcher. This version has a palmered body and a white-tipped natural grey squirrel hair wing instead of the original grey feather.

The Morning Glory excels as a loch fly on difficult, sunny days when its colours are illuminated to the full.

MORNING GLORY

HOOK: Size 8–12

THREAD: Black

TAIL: Blue cock hackle fibres

BODY: Flat gold tinsel

BODY HACKLE: Dyed-orange cock hackle

RIB: Fine oval gold tinsel

WING: Natural grey squirrel

trebles in a twist

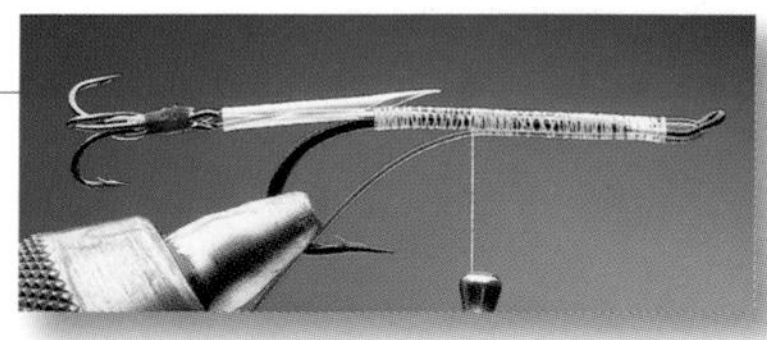

- Many sea-trout flies are dressed with flying trebles but they can carry an inherent fault. If the link from the front hook to the trailing treble is too flexible, the treble will tangle with the front hook during casting. Sea-trout fishing can be exasperating at the best of times without the nagging fear that the fly has neatly neutered itself in the dark.

  There is a simple solution guaranteed to prevent twist. The active ingredient is a length of polythene tubing (0.50mm inside diameter; 0.86mm outside diameter) of the kind used as cannula tubing in hospitals. It is also sold as lining for tube-flies.

- Prepare the flying treble in the usual way with 15–20lb nylon. Cut a length of tubing to suit the distance between the treble and the front hook. Taper one end to a steep angle. Bind the mono to the shaft of the hook, taking one end through the eye and back down the shaft. Secure the tapered end of the plastic tubing to the hook shaft with a last few turns of thread. Now tie the dressing as usual.

RELATED SUBJECT:

- Dyeing feathers p66

Dark Mackerel
From the North

A top-class sea-trout pattern, this is at its most effective when fished in the peat-stained waters of north-west Scotland. The claret hackles and dark, bronze mallard wing combine beautifully with the red tinsel to give a subdued sparkle that would be difficult to achieve with any other range of materials.

Claret is a great colour for dark days, whether the quarry is sea trout, salmon or brown trout, but there is another variation of the Dark Mackerel that is tied by substituting brown or furnace cock hackles for the claret coloured ones.

The collar hackle can be tied before or after the wing, but applying a long-fibred hackle afterwards does impart some extra movement to the fly, helped by using either hen or a soft-fibred cock hackle.

The Dark Mackerel should never be over-dressed because, as a point-fly, it needs to sink.

DARK MACKEREL

HOOK: Size 8–14 wet-fly

THREAD: Black

TAIL: Golden pheasant tippet

BODY: Flat, red tinsel

BODY HACKLE: Claret cock hackle

RIB: Copper wire

COLLAR HACKLE: Claret hen or soft-fibred cock hackle

WING: Bronze mallard

Connemara Black
From the West

This classic Irish pattern takes its name from a rugged part of that country once world-famous for its superb white trout (sea trout) fishing. The fly is basically a dark fly with a black body and hackle plus a wing of bronze mallard to give it a very dense silhouette. This overall colour is contrasted by a flash of orange at the tail plus a few fibres of blue jay at the throat to create this very dark, handsome fly.

This combination makes the Connemara Black a deadly lake fly for both salmon and sea trout.

Though the original version of this pattern is tied, as here, with a tag of orange floss, this is often omitted. In another minor variation, jungle-cock cheeks are added: this variation is a noted killer on Lough Currane.

CONNEMARA BLACK

HOOK: Size 8–14 wet-fly

THREAD: Black

TAG: Orange floss

TAIL: Golden-pheasant topping

BODY: Black seal's fur

RIB: Fine oval silver tinsel

HACKLE: Black cock hackle with a few fibres of blue jay

WING: Bronze mallard

Sea Trout from the Salt

Sea trout are more than willing to feed in salt water

Sea trout are present all year round in our estuaries and inshore waters – even if a river isn't known for a run of sea trout, the chances are they will still be found in its estuary – and they prefer to feast on eels, be they true sand eels or migrating elvers.

The reason for almost every failure to catch salt-water sea trout is because the attempts have been made at the wrong time of the tide. Most estuaries fish best in the first hour of a rising tide when the freshwater is running through a narrow channel and both sea trout and sand eels are confined to a small area. Keep just ahead of the incoming tide, casting the lure along the edge of the moving water. A word of warning: some estuaries are very wide and the incoming tide races across the sand like a frightened horse, possibly cutting off any means of reaching higher and safer ground.

How the lure is retrieved is crucial. You might think that sand eels

GOLDEN-OLIVE SAND EEL

HOOK: Size 10–18 salmon double

THREAD: Fire orange

BODY: Gold Mylar holographic tinsel

RIB: Fine gold wire

HACKLE: Golden-olive cock fibres

WING: White bucktail, White Pearl Sparkle Flash, golden-olive bucktail, Yellow Pearl Sparkle Flash and peacock herl

EYES: Small gold adhesive decals covered with clear varnish and epoxy resin glue

TYING THE GOLDEN-OLIVE SAND EEL

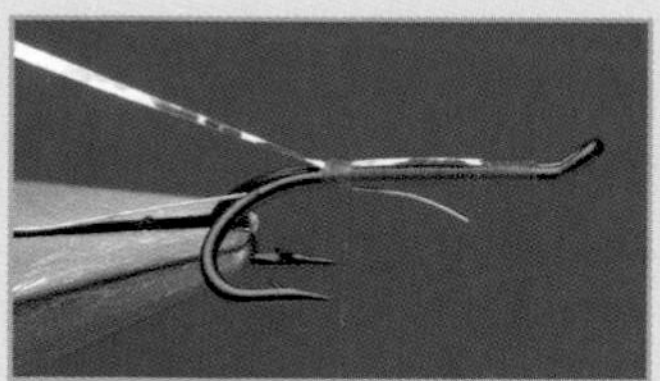

1 Run the tying thread in touching turns to a point above the hook point. Tie in the gold wire and holographic tinsel.

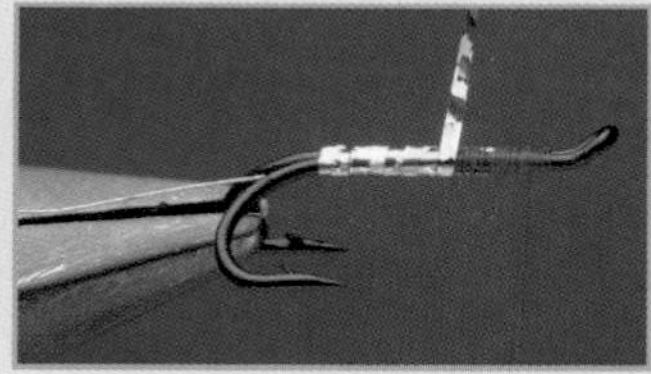

2 Take the thread back to a point near the eye and start to wind the gold holographic tinsel.

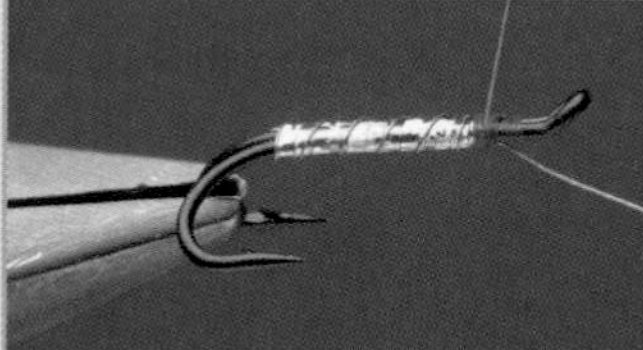

3 Complete the body and secure the tinsel. Trim away the waste tinsel.

5 Secure the golden-olive bucktail fibres and trim away the unwanted ends.

6 Tie in three or four peacock herls to reach past the other wing materials.

7 Build up the head into a smooth cone and add the decal eyes one at a time with turns of the tying thread. Secure with clear varnish or epoxy glue.

RELATED SUBJECT:
• Fish imitations p96

wriggle away like mad things. Not so: they drift around like little dark sticks, their direction controlled by the pulses of the tide. Patience is the key to the whole thing. The fly should be cast across the flow and left to the mercy of the tide to move this way and that – just like the live sand eel. The method does take some getting used to, the temptation to retrieve the lure at speed being difficult to resist at times. Takes are usually solid affairs, but there are times when all you'll feel is a slight tug as the sea trout attempts to disable the eel. Ignore such early warnings: it is rare for the sea trout, or one of its travelling companions, not to make a second, more positive, attempt.

The sand eel is very slim, the back is a darkish olive and the belly a greenish silver. Use the minimum of materials or the desired slimness will be lost. Lures with long and mobile wings bring with them the annoying habit of wrapping themselves round the hook. This doesn't happen as frequently if the glittery stuff is sandwiched between strands of bucktail. Tying the lure on a heavy, short-shanked double hook not only helps to overcome this problem but the extra weight counterbalances the buoyancy of the materials, helping the fly swim on an even keel.

While the 2–3in lure is the one most commonly used, it pays to have some a little longer ready for the day when the sea-trout lock on to the jumbo sand eels. Tie the 2–3in version on a size 10, and anything longer on a size 8.

The eyes are an important feature. The simple decal kind can be fixed on with the tying thread.

4 Tie in a bunch of golden-olive cock hackle fibres.

8 The finished Golden-Olive Sand Eel.

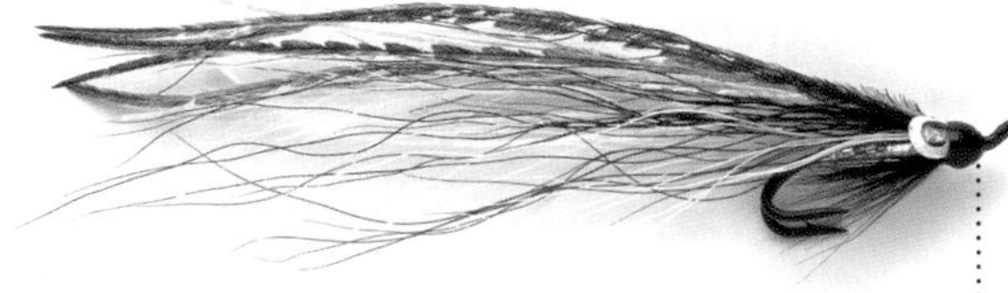

AMERICAN SMELT

HOOK: Size 10–18 salmon double

BODY: Silver Mylar holographic tinsel

RIB: Fine silver wire

HACKLE: Black cock hackle fibres

WING: Red bucktail, White Pearl Sparkle Flash, white bucktail, UV Multi Pearl Sparkle Flash, black bucktail, peacock herl

EYES: Small silver decals

BLUE AND SILVER SAND EEL

HOOK: Size 10–12 salmon double

THREAD: Fire red

BODY: Silver Mylar holographic tinsel

RIB: Fine silver wire

HACKLE: Teal blue cock

WING: White bucktail, White Pearl, UV Blue Pearl Sparkle Flash, blue bucktail, peacock herl

EYES: Small silver decals

Ally's Shrimp – the Original and Best

A salmon fly so successful, it can be fished with confidence on rivers worldwide

In the August 1988 issue of *Trout and Salmon*, Alastair Gowans revealed his latest creation – the Ally's Shrimp – to the salmon-fishing world.

Little did he realize, then, what an impact it would have. In his article Alastair wrote: 'It is worth a try any time from late spring to late autumn, and fish have been taken on it from the Dee, Tay, Tummel, Tweed and Esks.' Since then the Ally's Shrimp has probably taken fish from every salmon-producing river in the world.

Alastair Gowans' intention was to produce an illusion of something 'shrimpy' and semi-translucent, like the creatures he had caught while on board a trawler fishing the Minch.

As with any fly (particularly a salmon fly) it is a fact that the more people who fish a particular pattern, the greater the number of fish that will be caught on it, but the Ally's Shrimp is something special, and few fishers would admit to never having fished the fly at one time or another. The original fly has spawned a host of colour variants: the Yellow Ally's Shrimp is perhaps the most successful.

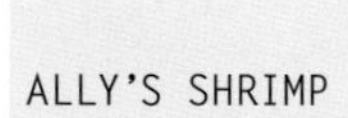

ALLY'S SHRIMP

HOOK: Treble, double in sizes to suit conditions

THREAD: Red

TAIL: Small bunch of hot-orange bucktail, twice the length of the hook shank

RIB: Oval silver tinsel

BODY: Rear half red floss; front half black floss

UNDERWING: Natural grey squirrel tail

OVERWING: Golden pheasant tippets

BEARD HACKLE: Natural grey squirrel tail

HACKLE: Long hot-orange cock

HEAD: Red varnish

just one pattern

Some valuable advice from Crawford Little, writing in *Trout and Salmon* magazine.

Q: If you had to fish with just one pattern of salmon fly, in a range of sizes, which one would it be?

A: From May to September in Scotland, it would probably be the Ally's Shrimp. But, taking the season as a whole, I would have to plump for the Willie Gunn. Would either of these restrictions significantly reduce my catches? Given that I am to be allowed a range of sizes, I doubt it. But it would be like having to eat the same food day after day. Nourishing perhaps, but not very interesting.

RELATED SUBJECT:

- Dyeing feathers p66

1 Fix the hook in the vice and run the thread down to the bend. Wind on three or four turns of fine oval silver tinsel to form a tag. At the front of the tag catch in a long, thin bunch of orange bucktail.

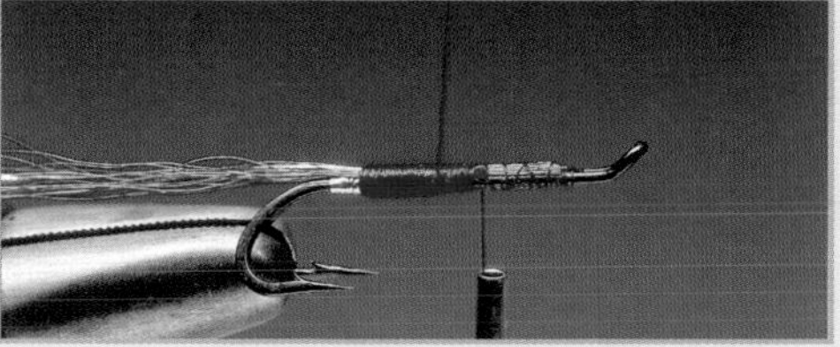

2 Wind the tying thread over the waste ends of the bucktail to form an even base for the body. Halfway along the shank catch in 4in of red floss.

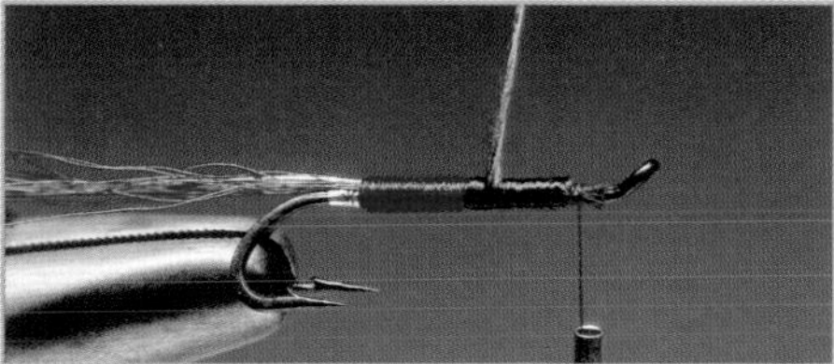

3 Wind the red floss in close turns down to the base of the tail. Wind it back again to its catching-in point, forming a double layer that helps create a smooth effect. Repeat with black floss to just behind the eye and tie off.

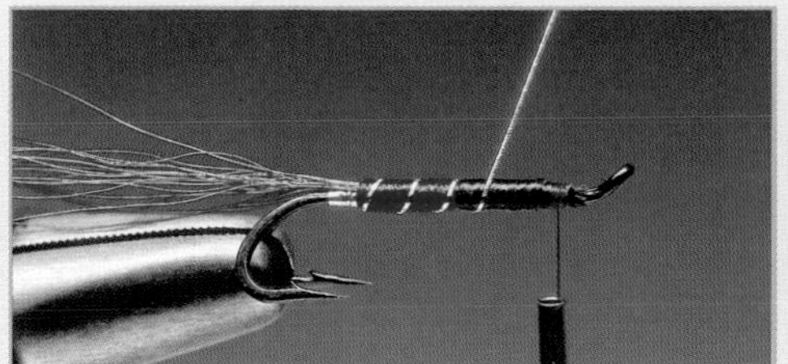

4 Take hold of the silver tinsel and wind it over the body in six evenly spaced turns. Tie and remove end.

5 Rotate the jaws and catch in a slim bunch of grey squirrel tail to form a beard hackle. Rotate back and catch in a second bunch of squirrel tail to form a wing.

6 Tie in a medium-sized golden pheasant tippet feather at the front of the wing so that it sits flat. Now catch in a soft-fibred orange cock hackle by its base and wind on three or four full turns.

7 Secure the loose end of the hackle and remove the excess. Stroke the hackle fibres back over the body and position with thread. Build a neat head and cast off with a whip finish.

Summer Salmon

Slim and deadly for bright skies and thin water

The Executioner

Anyone trying to incorporate the deadliest colours for salmon and sea trout would probably find something like the Executioner coming to mind. This striking pattern combines black, red and silver, set off by cheeks of jungle cock.

The pattern owes much to the Silver Stoat, another great fly for migratory fish, but the flash of fluorescent red floss gives it a distinct edge. The ratio of red to silver may be varied: the red can be little more than a butt or extend up to half the body length.

Being used specifically for summer work, the Executioner is tied relatively small on doubles and trebles ranging from size 6 down to 12. Dyed-black squirrel tail is the preferred material for the wing. Having a soft, fine texture, this hair provides greater mobility than bucktail on small flies.

The Executioner is usually fished singly on a floating line, but it also works well as a point fly with the addition of a simple hackled fly such as a Black Pennel on the dropper.

EXECUTIONER

HOOK: Size 6–12 doubles and trebles
THREAD: Black
TAG: Fine oval silver tinsel
TAIL: Golden-pheasant crest
BODY: *(rear section)*: Fluorescent red floss; *(front section)*: Flat silver tinsel
RIB: Oval silver tinsel
HACKLE: Black cock hackle
WING: Dyed-black squirrel tail
CHEEKS: Jungle cock

The Editor

'Slim and deadly' might describe its creator, Sandy Leventon, then editor of *Trout and Salmon*. The Editor first made its impact on the River Spey in the late 1980s. Since then it has proved a deadly pattern for salmon and grilse (and sea trout) in rivers at home and abroad. Few fishers on the Tweed in late spring and early summer are without one or two in their boxes.

The pearly body, fluorescent rib and jungle cock cheeks really gleam in the water. In any river carrying a slight peat stain the Editor stands out like a beacon. It seems to do best on a sparkling day of sunshine and high cloud.

Although devised primarily as a fly for late spring and early summer, when a flashy pattern with plenty of blue in it seems particularly attractive to fresh fish, the Editor is also a great fly for many autumn rivers. Tied on a big single hook or a tube, it has produced great catches on the Tweed, Tay and Tyne. It may be tied as a double (in sizes 4–8 for the Spey in May), or on singles, tubes and Waddingtons (see opposite). The wing should be at least one-and-a half times the length of the hook shank.

EDITOR

HOOK: To suit conditions
THREAD: Black
UNDERBODY: White Antron
BODY: Pearl lurex
RIB: Fluorescent-green nylon
HACKLE: Blue cock
WING: Black bucktail
CHEEKS: Jungle cock

RELATED SUBJECT:
- Barbless solutions p131

waddingtons and doubles

- Catch-and-release measures on many rivers require the use of barbless double hooks. These cannot be slipped on to a Waddington shank in the usual way because the hooks would hang to one side of the shank. Does this mean that Waddingtons can't be used for spring fishing? Many anglers are devoted to flies tied on Waddington shanks.

  There is no reason for you to give up on Waddingtons. Introduce a small split ring between the shank and the eye of the double hook. This ensures that the hook sits in line with the shank. As a bonus, if you damage the hook, a replacement can be slipped on to the split ring.

  The components in the photograph top right are a 1¾in Waddington shank, a 5mm split ring and a size 8 Partridge Big Mouth Double. For shorter shanks, you can use a smaller split ring. Mustad make them in sizes down to 3mm. The whole thing is kept in line with a short length of silicon rubber extension tubing, which is soft and pliable enough to fit over the eye of the hook, split-ring and shank, and still flexible enough to avoid any leverage when a fish is hooked.

A Waddington shank and double hook attached with a split ring. Note the short length of tubing pushed down the shank of the double hook.

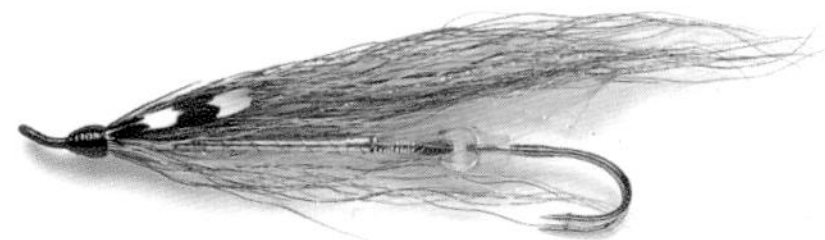

Perfectly aligned: the extension tubing has been pushed up to cover the eye of the hook, the split ring and the loop on the Waddington shank.

Irish Shrimps

Patterns that pulsate with life

In the continual search for the elusive killer pattern, tried and trusted colour combinations are often melded with successful profiles or shapes. Irish shrimp patterns are renowned for the 'life' they show in the water, thanks to the three rings of feather fibre at tail, middle and head. The Silver Wilkinson was a famous 19th-century fully dressed salmon fly from the days of complex built-wings and exotic materials. The original called for strands of summer duck, light mottled turkey and florican bustard. It had the distinction of being one of the very first salmon flies to be tied with a tinsel body.

The Wilkinson Shrimp is an Irish-style shrimp derivation of the Silver Wilkinson. It dispenses with the wing and merely has a body of silver tinsel plus the magenta and blue hackles, which impart the colour of the original. Rather than tying the hackles at the throat, they are applied separately, the magenta hackle dividing the body in two and the blue hackle used as a collar. To complete the transformation into an Irish Shrimp pattern, a red golden-pheasant breast feather is wound at the bend to suggest the feelers of a natural shrimp and to add some mobility to the fly.

This pattern is known as a Light Wilkinson Shrimp and is a great fly for tempting fresh fish in bright conditions. A variation on the theme, the Dark Wilkinson Shrimp, is tied in a similar style but with a middle hackle of rich, kingfisher blue and a claret hackle at the collar.

The Wilkinson Shrimp works well on a variety of water types. Not only is it a great fly for the river, it is also a

WILKINSON SHRIMP

HOOK: Size 4–10 single, double or treble
THREAD: Red
TAG: Oval silver tinsel
TAIL: Red golden pheasant breast feather
BODY: Flat silver tinsel
RIB: Oval silver tinsel
MIDDLE HACKLE: Dyed-magenta cock hackle
COLLAR HACKLE: Blue cock hackle
WINGS: Jungle cock
HEAD: Red varnish

TYING THE WILKINSON SHRIMP

1 Run the tying thread down to the bend. Catch in the rib of fine oval silver tinsel. Wind on four turns for the tag, secure the loose end and trim. Take a large, red, golden pheasant breast feather. Catch in by its tip just in front of the tag.

2 Wind the feather round the shank. Stroke the fibres back on each turn so they project over the hook bend. Secure and trim. Catch in the oval silver tinsel rib. Take the thread halfway along the shank in close turns, covering the waste end of the tinsel. Catch in a tapered point of the flat silver tinsel.

3 Wind the tinsel down the shank in touching (but not overlapping) turns. Keeping under tension, wind to tail then back to form a double layer. Secure and trim. Wind the oval tinsel over it in three, evenly spaced turns. Secure and trim.

RELATED SUBJECT: • Dyeing feathers p66

noted fish-taker on Irish loughs. Especially effective for fresh fish, particularly spring salmon, its light tones make it an ideal fly to try in bright conditions when the river is still carrying a little colour.

Fishing the River Owenea, Co. Donegal, Ireland

tip

- To set jungle-cock feathers precisely at the cheeks of a fly, tie them in pointing over the eye and with the poorer sides facing outwards. After tying the wing or hackle in place, fold back the jungle-cock feathers and secure.

4 Catch in a dyed-magenta cock hackle in front of the first body section. Wind on three full turns, closely butted together. Secure and trim. Stroke the fibres back over the body then catch in more oval tinsel rib and repeat the body-building sequence from steps 2 and 3.

5 Select a matched pair of jungle cock feathers and place them back-to-back a short distance from the eye. Catch in a dyed-blue hackle just behind the eye to form the collar. The fibres of this hackle should be slightly shorter than those of the magenta middle hackle.

6 Build a neat head with the tying thread before casting it off with a whip finish. Add two coats of red varnish to the head to complete.

Black and Yellow

Black and yellow have always made an attention-grabbing combination in nature

Several effective flies draw on the strident combination of black and yellow to attract the notice of spring salmon. Both these Scottish flies have a sterling reputation in their home waters. Most Scottish fisherman carry a Munro Killer and both flies are becoming increasingly popular on Irish rivers.

Tosh

The Tosh is an extremely simple pattern to tie. Sometimes referred to simply as the Black and Yellow, it takes its name from the dog that provided the black hair for that first fly in 1957 when Mr E Ritchie, the pattern's inventor (and Tosh's owner) was a gillie on the Delfur beat of the Spey.

The present-day version of the Tosh is tied in a wide range of sizes, from large tubes and Waddingtons down to small doubles and trebles. In the smaller sizes, dyed squirrel tail is favoured over the coarser bucktail. Either way the wing should be tied long – at least one-and-a half times that of the body to give the fly plenty of movement in the water.

The hackle should also be quite long. It can be tied with dyed-yellow cock hackle fibres or with dyed hair, either bucktail or squirrel tail, though some tyers prefer the crinkly texture of calf tail.

Some versions of the Tosh are now tied with a tail and a rib (see page 123), but the original lacks both and, apart from that flash of yellow at the throat, it is uncompromisingly black.

The Tosh, in its variety of sizes and weights, works well throughout the season but is particularly noted as a killer during spring and early summer. Its dark tones make it a very good pattern for clear water.

TOSH

HOOK: **To suit conditions**

THREAD: **Black**

BODY: **Black floss**

HACKLE: **Yellow hair or hackle fibres**

WING: **Black bucktail or squirrel tail**

double chance

- You can alter the size, weight or colour of a tube-fly by slipping two flies, one behind the other, on the leader. You can extend this trick using other elements and microtubes (see p130).

Munro Killer

The Munro Killer is considered by many experienced anglers to be the best of all modern Scottish salmon flies and is one of only a handful of dressings that might be regarded as indispensable. It is a noted pattern for the Spey and may be tied on doubles, trebles plus Waddingtons and tubes when early conditions dictate the need for a big fly.

Black, yellow and orange make a deadly colour combination for salmon and the Munro Killer uses this to good effect with a bi-coloured hair wing contrasting with a bright orange hackle at the throat.

Some aficionados vary the proportion of the colours in the wing and hackle to suit conditions, incorporating more black for use in clear water and more orange and yellow for autumn. It is an extremely versatile pattern that will take fish throughout the season.

The key to tying this pattern is to keep the wing long and not too heavy so that it has plenty of mobility. Wing length should be up to twice the length of the body.

MUNRO KILLER

HOOK: To suit conditions

THREAD: Black

TAG: Oval gold tinsel

BODY: Black floss

RIB: Oval gold tinsel

HACKLE: Orange cock hackle fibres under dyed blue

WING: Black hair over a small amount of yellow hair

Grilse taken on a small shrimp fly, with a selection of low-water flies

A Cascade of Salmon Flies

Celebrity in salmon flies comes and goes. Some favourites – Willie Gunn, Munro Killer, Hairy Mary, Stoat's Tail and so on – will always have a place in anglers' fly boxes

One of the biggest changes in fly design came when Alastair Gowans produced his famous Ally's Shrimp (see pages 112–113). This fly and its variants must have taken countless thousands of fish since its invention, and it is used worldwide. It is rare to find someone who does not have at least one Ally's Shrimp in his box. Indeed many fishers seldom use anything else.

Interestingly, in recent years Ally's other famous pattern, the Cascade, seems to have overtaken the Ally's Shrimp in popularity. Many salmon anglers now swear by this pattern. The attraction of these long-tailed dressings to salmon is unquestionable, and the use of modern flashy materials such as Crystal Hair adds that bit of sparkle and translucence that catches the eye.

The most important feature of the Cascade is its overall shape and long tail, which gives a more lifelike movement in the current, something that standard dressings can't do. Furthermore, the long tail creates a bit of buoyancy and keeps the fly on an even keel as it swims and hovers through the stream. This keeps the fly looking 'alive' from the moment it lands in the water until it is lifted off. This surely is an ideal style of dressing for salmon flies.

Ally Gowans didn't just come up with a new pattern when he produced the Cascade. He created a new style of dressing a fly, a style that changed the behaviour of the fly in the water – and this is the key to the Cascade's success.

The spectacular ascendance of these new flies has eclipsed many of the older, more traditional patterns. But the Jock Scott, Thunder and Lightning and Garry Dog have taken too many salmon to be forgotten. These old salmon flies have colour and glitter combinations that have been tried and trusted over countless seasons. Why not tie these patterns and combinations 'Cascade style'?

Many of them are ideal for this style. They have a good blend of colours that can make a fly 'glow' in the water. It is just a matter of picking some colours from the wing to use as a long tail, adding some Crystal Hair material, and the rest falls into place. The variations for this style are endless.

Ally's original dressings may not be bettered, but it is always fun trying something different, and these long-tailed 'Cascade style' flies certainly look good in the water.

Here are some favourites. They can be tied on doubles, trebles, or even copper or brass tubes for heavy sunk-line spring and autumn fishing.

tip

- The tails on all these dressings should be long and slim. For example, a fly tied on a size 6 Esmond Drury treble could be around 3in long. When two or three colours are required for the tail, they can be rolled between the fingers to mix them, or put one colour on top of the other with Crystal Hair on top: two strands are enough for most conditions.

CASCADE

It is given to few men to create an acknowledged classic salmon fly. Ally Gowans has created two. Shown here is a simplified Cascade with silver Mylar body.

HOOK: Copper tube

THREAD: Black

BODY: Silver Mylar holographic piping with white thread tag

TAIL: Mixed yellow and orange bucktail and four strands of pearl Crystal Hair, extending twice the length of the tube

WING: Black squirrel tail and four strands of pearl Crystal Hair

HACKLE: Four turns each of long yellow and orange cock hackle

HEAD: Varnished black thread

JOCK SCOTT

This is possibly the best-known 'classic' pattern. What would the old traditional built-wing fly-dressers think of this cascade version?

TAIL: Yellow, red and blue bucktail and two strands of pearl Crystal Hair

BODY: *(rear half)*: yellow floss; *(front half)*: black floss

RIB: Oval silver

WING: Brown hair as for Dusty Miller with two strands pearl Crystal Hair

HACKLE: Black cock or hen with one turn natural grey guinea-fowl in front

HEAD: Black

DUSTY MILLER

This is a famous old fly but seldom seen these days. Dress it on big tubes for early spring, or doubles and trebles for the rest of the season right through to late autumn.

TAIL: Slim long bunch of yellow, red and orange bucktail with two strands of pearl Crystal Hair (use mirror flash on large tubes)

BODY: *(rear half)* silver tinsel; *(front half)* orange floss

RIB: Oval silver tinsel

WING: Brown hair from centre of orange bucktail (this is a good substitute for bronze mallard but not all orange tails have it) and two strands pearl Crystal Hair

HACKLE: Golden-olive cock or hen with one turn natural grey guinea-fowl in front

HEAD: Black

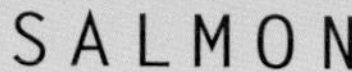

GARRY DOG

This has always been a favourite spring and autumn fly tied on big Waddingtons and tubes. Try this style on a treble or double hook for lighter work or coloured water.

TAIL: Red bucktail with yellow bucktail on top and two strands of silver Crystal Hair

BODY: *(rear half):* silver tinsel; *(front half):* black floss

RIB: Oval silver

WING: Black squirrel with two strands of silver Crystal Hair

HACKLE: Blue guinea-fowl

HEAD: Black

GREEN HIGHLANDER

This one is slowly becoming more popular. It should be. Dressed with a long tail it is a very attractive fly. Good in large sizes fished deep in the spring.

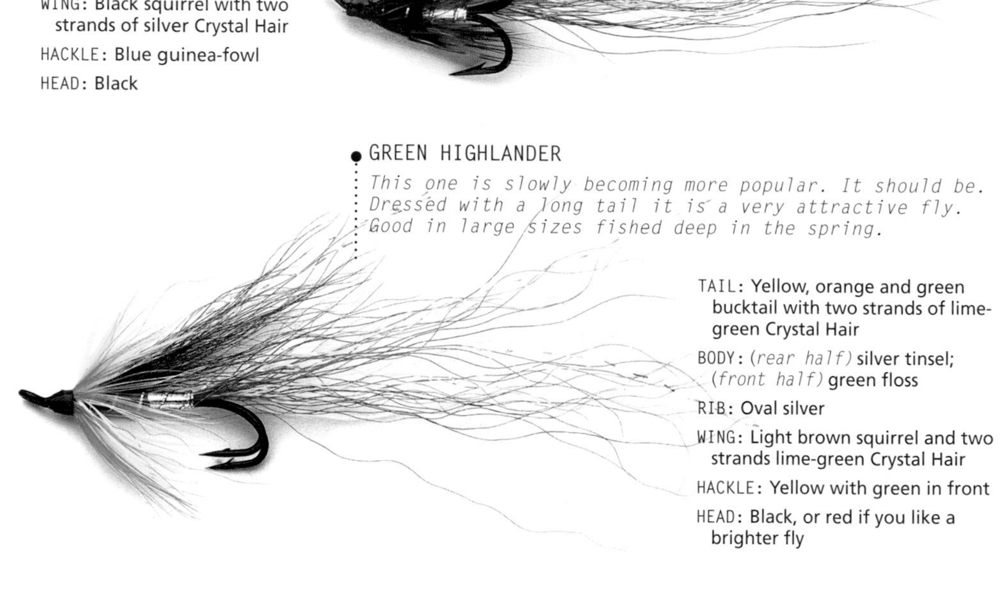

TAIL: Yellow, orange and green bucktail with two strands of lime-green Crystal Hair

BODY: *(rear half)* silver tinsel; *(front half)* green floss

RIB: Oval silver

WING: Light brown squirrel and two strands lime-green Crystal Hair

HACKLE: Yellow with green in front

HEAD: Black, or red if you like a brighter fly

THUNDER AND LIGHTNING

This famous fly needs no introduction, but try tying it this way.

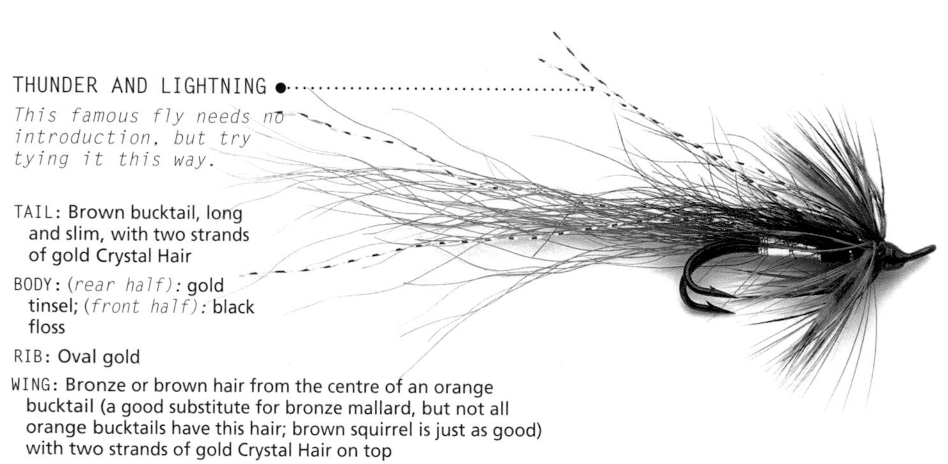

TAIL: Brown bucktail, long and slim, with two strands of gold Crystal Hair

BODY: *(rear half):* gold tinsel; *(front half):* black floss

RIB: Oval gold

WING: Bronze or brown hair from the centre of an orange bucktail (a good substitute for bronze mallard, but not all orange bucktails have this hair; brown squirrel is just as good) with two strands of gold Crystal Hair on top

HACKLE: Orange cock or hen with one turn of blue guinea-fowl wound in front

HEAD: Black

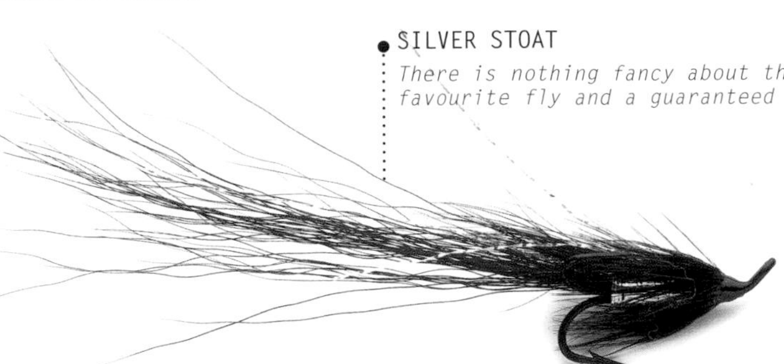

SILVER STOAT

There is nothing fancy about this fly. It is simply a favourite fly and a guaranteed fish-catcher all season.

TAIL: Black bucktail with two strands of pearl Crystal Hair

BODY: Silver tinsel

RIB: Oval silver

WING: Black squirrel and pearl Crystal Hair

HACKLE: Black cock or hen

HEAD: Black

TOSH

This was originally tied with a black body and no rib (see page 118) - but try it with a silver body in sizes 8, 10 and 12 when the grilse are running.

TAIL: Yellow bucktail with black on top and two strands of silver Crystal Hair

BODY: *(rear half)* silver tinsel; *(front half)* black floss

WING: Black squirrel and silver Crystal Hair

RIB: Oval silver

HACKLE: Yellow cock or hen

HEAD: Black

SILVER DOCTOR

Tie this one on brass or copper tubes for early spring. This is an excellent fly for fishing deep on those days when snow and ice are numbing your hands and feet.

TAIL: Red, blue and yellow bucktail with two strands of pearl Crystal Mirror Flash

BODY: Silver tinsel, or Mylar tubing for tubes

RIB: Oval silver or two coats varnish for Mylar tubing

WING: Grey squirrel and two strands pearl Crystal Mirror Flash

HACKLE: Blue cock or hen with natural grey guinea-fowl in front

HEAD: Red varnish

tip

- The new Veniard's Crystal Mirror Flash is a very flashy material and it looks good on the larger sizes. The wing should be tied in a little further back than usual so that space is left for the hackles to be wound in front of the wing. The shape created by this method contributes much to this style of fly's attraction. Make sure there is room behind the eye of the hook for a Double Turle Knot. Not every hook manufacturer puts a proper neck on the eye of their salmon hooks.

Willie Gunn

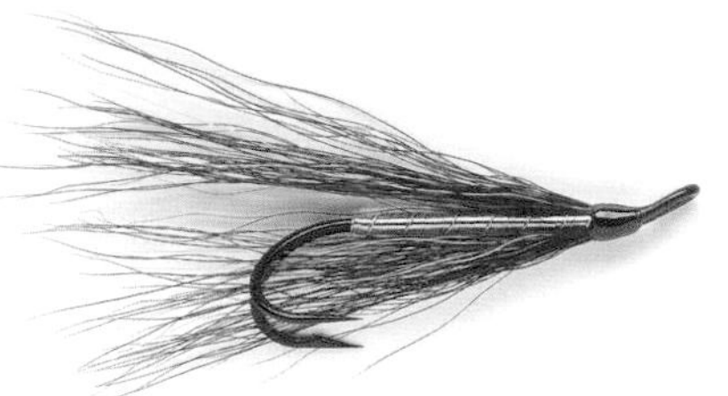

The man and the myth behind the world's best Atlantic salmon fly

The Willie Gunn is arguably the most successful salmon fly ever invented. It has probably caught more Atlantic salmon all over the world than any other fly.

It is attributed to Rob Wilson, the celebrated salmon fisher and proprietor of the tackle shop in Brora, Sutherland – although the story goes that it was actually created by an RAF officer, Flight Lieutenant 'Dusty' Miller, who tied flies for Rob Wilson. Wilson and Miller were trying to simplify some of the hundreds of complicated and expensive full-dressed flies favoured in the late 1940s. Some of the rare and exotic materials for these fancy creations were becoming hard to obtain in wartime. One of the new patterns was a variation, tied solely from hair, of a Thunder and Lightning, a famous pattern that had reliably been catching Highland salmon for a century.

At the time, Willie Gunn worked as a gillie and chauffeur on the Brora River. He visited Rob's shop and went through all the new salmon flies, choosing one that took his fancy, which Rob immediately christened the 'Willie Gunn'.

GOLD-BODIED WILLIE GUNN

HOOK: To suit conditions: single, double and treble hooks, tubes and Waddingtons

THREAD: Black

BODY: Flat gold tinsel

RIB: Medium oval gold tinsel

WING: Mixture of red, black, orange and yellow bucktail. Squirrel is more suitable for the smaller flies

Fishing the River Awe, Scotland

In the hands of its namesake, the Willie Gunn proved astonishingly successful on its first outings, and soon the fly's fame spread throughout the Highlands and beyond.

The original Willie Gunn had a black floss body ribbed with gold, but the pattern featured here, with a gold body, seems to be even more popular these days. Many fishers believe that the addition of jungle-cock cheeks on the bigger versions for sunk-line fishing improves it even further.

tips

- Fish it with confidence on any river where Atlantic salmon swim, and never be without one on any Scottish river.
- Tied as tubes or Waddingtons for spring and autumn fishing, and down to size 12–14 singles or doubles for summer, the Willie Gunn is truly a fly for all seasons.

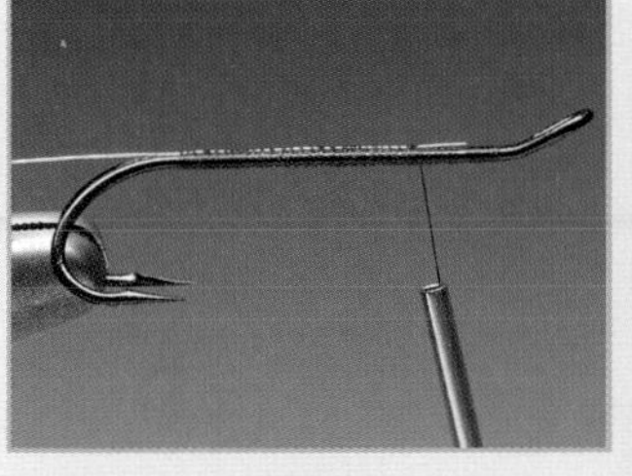

1 Run the tying thread on at the eye. Carry it down the shank in close turns and catch in 3in of oval gold tinsel at the bend. Wind the tying thread back up the shank, covering the waste end of the tinsel.

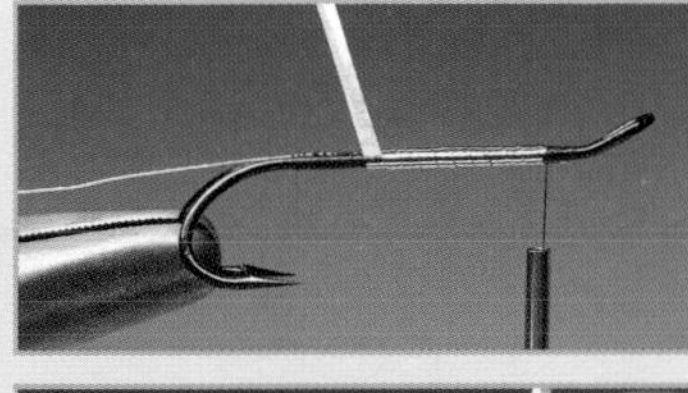

2 Just behind the eye, tie in 4in of flat gold tinsel, cut to a point, with tight turns. Wind the tinsel down the shank in close turns without overlapping.

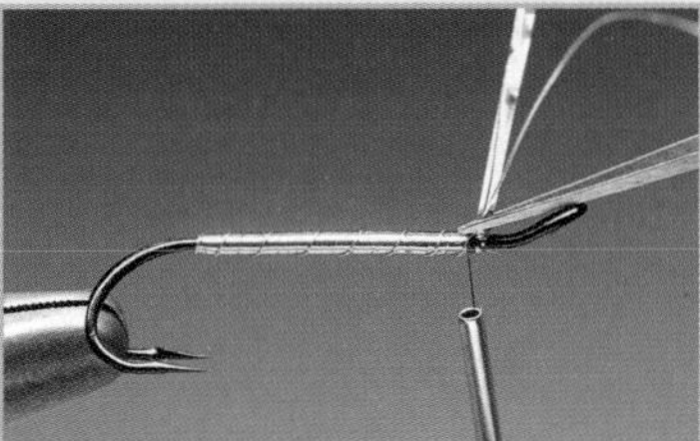

3 Wind the flat tinsel back up the shank. This double layer creates a very smooth effect. Secure the loose end of the flat tinsel then wind the oval gold tinsel rib over the body in evenly spaced turns. Secure and remove all excess tinsel.

4 Take four equal bunches of black, orange, red and yellow bucktail. Place the hair in the palm of your hand and carefully blend them together with your fingers until the colours are well mixed and the tips level. Divide the mixed bunch of hair into two equal bunches then invert the hook in the vice. Catch one bunch of hair in place so that the tips project well past the hook bend.

5 Return the hook to its original position. Catch in the second bunch, ensuring the tips of both bunches are level. Work the hair evenly around the hook and secure with tight thread turns.

Small is Beautiful

A tiny Microtube is just the thing to tempt the grilse of high summer

It has long been accepted that summer grilse prefer tiny flies. Grilse will rarely refuse a tiny tube armed with size 14 or even smaller treble hook. By tiny, I mean scraps of tube ¼–½in long. For patterns, 'miniaturize' your favourite tube flies, concentrating on the basic colours only and doing away with non-essentials. Remember: you've got less than ½in of tube to play with, and that includes the head. The result is a sparkling little creation that darts about in the current no more than an inch or so beneath the surface – and that's just about perfect for grilse lying in shallow water. If the current brings the tube to the surface, making it skate, swap it for a similar fly dressed on a bit of aluminium or copper tube.

Such short lengths of tube are hard to buy so you'll have to make your own. If you're using plastic tube, cut off a little more than the length required and bring the end of the tube up slowly to a flame and the edge will curl over nicely, leaving a little lip. While you can use the usual clear plastic tubing, I much prefer the white cotton-bud sort, which acts like a white base undercoat, reflecting any colours wound over it.

Making the aluminium and copper tubes is a little trickier. Remove the plastic inner lining from the tube before cutting and then slide it back after smoothing the edges of the metal.

To avoid the tiny tubes looking like an unsightly blob, be as mean as sin with the materials, and make every turn of tying thread count. On bigger flies, you can use the thread to correct little mistakes in the tying, but on tubes this small, every single turn must achieve something, either to secure a material or to provide a colour.

The wing needs the most restraint. Ten fine tips trimmed from the bottom part of a bucktail are ample. But whatever hair you use, if you can't see the body quite clearly through the hairs, remove the wing and start again. These tiny tubes lend themselves beautifully to any of the shrimp-type dressings. However, as you have so little room to play with, it is easier to tie the fibres in evenly around the tube rather than to wind the whole feather as you would with a larger fly. The body is nothing more than a few turns of tying thread, tinsel, and a ribbing of the finest wire you can find. Although they may not be included in the original dressing, tiny jungle-cock cheeks add something to the tiny tubes.

RED SHRIMP MICROTUBE

THREAD: Red

TAG: Silver

TAIL: Dyed-red golden pheasant rump feather

RIB: Silver wire

BODY: Red thread

HACKLE: Badger cock

CHEEKS: Jungle cock

HEAD: Red

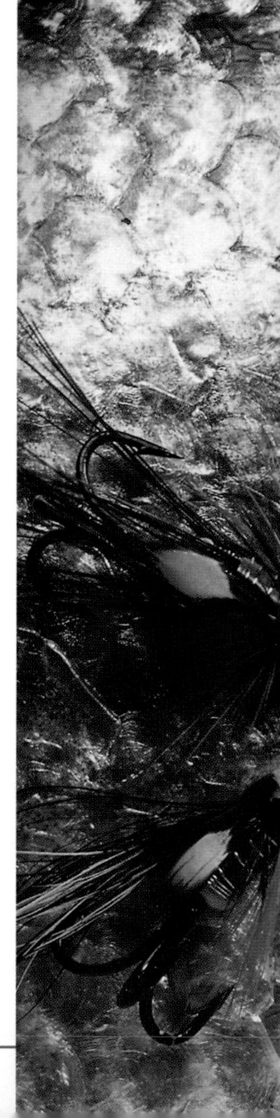

RELATED SUBJECT:
• Tube combinations p130

tip

- Make a little tube fly by using a stainless steel crimp used by sea anglers. The treble hook is held in place by a short length of plastic tubing.

Alive and Kicking

Mobile wings and coneheads combine to put life into salmon flies

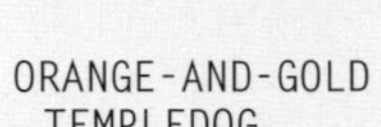

Out in the main flow of a boulder-strewn pool where the water is turbulent, there is enough natural movement in the fast current to work even a big, heavy fly like a standard hairwinged brass tube. Once the fly has completed its swing across the river, however, it usually meets slack water near the bank. Out of the main current, it is effectively dead. A salmon will often follow a fly almost to the bank but, without any natural movement in the fly to impart life, the fish will usually lose interest at this point.

What's needed is a fly with plenty of movement – one that will work in all current speeds, something with a soft, highly mobile wing. Combine this mobility with a weight near the front and instead of a fly that hangs lifelessly you produce a ducking, diving action that adds hugely to the fly's effectiveness.

Metal coneheads were originally used to create a weighted head. A recent development has been to position a conehead behind the wing of patterns with highly mobile wings, such as the Templedog. This not only adds weight, but the angled face of the cone elevates the wing, increasing its action in the water. It also means that a much smaller head can be formed.

ORANGE-AND-GOLD TEMPLEDOG

TUBE: Fluorescent orange Frödin tube – medium diameter

CONEHEAD: Medium-size gold tungsten

THREAD: Fluorescent orange

BODY: Gold holographic tinsel

RIB: Red wire

BASE WING: Dyed-red Arctic fox tail

MIDDLE WING: Orange and red soft-fibred cock hackles

OVERWING: Strands of pearl and gold Flashabou and dyed-orange Arctic fox tail

CHEEKS: Jungle cock

TYING THE ORANGE-AND-GOLD TEMPLEDOG

1 Stretch one end of warmed Frödin tube so that it becomes considerably thinner. Slide the conehead on to the tube to check the stretched end is thin enough. Trim both ends to length.

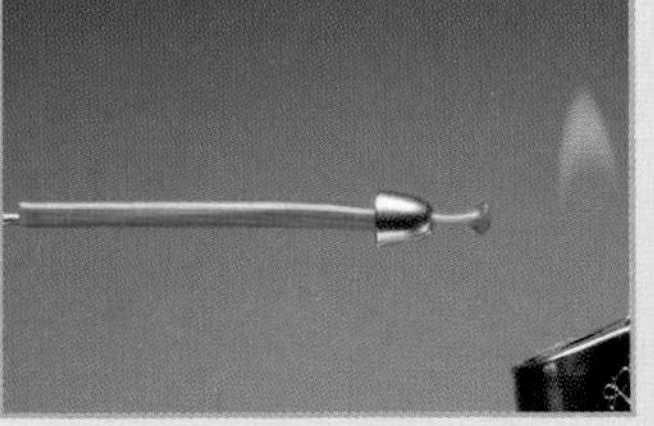

2 Apply a naked flame to the end of the tube so that it melts, forming a burred end. This stops the dressing slipping off. Tie on any body materials.

3 Push the cone back hard against the shoulder. In front of the cone, catch in a short length of Arctic fox tail so that it points forward.

RELATED SUBJECTS: • Using plastics p94 • Dyeing feathers p66

While it is possible to use ordinary tubing for this style of fly, a product developed by Mikael Frödin and marketed by Guideline Tackle makes this task much easier. Frödin tubes come in various colours, including fluorescent green, red and orange, and in several diameters. The larger diameters easily accommodate the eye of a treble or double hook without the need to add a silicone rubber sleeve. The greatest advantage of a Frödin tube is that it can be stretched, making one end thin enough to pass through the hole in a cone. Holding one end with pliers, simply stretch it in one steady pull – warming the tube in the steam of a kettle will help the process.

Now slide a conehead down the stretched section until it hits the shoulder left by the non-stretched tube. Trim both ends so that the body is the required length and there is a section of stretched tube in front of the cone long enough to accommodate the wing and hackle.

You can remove the cone and apply any body materials first – though with the coloured Frödin tubes this isn't always necessary: it's just a matter of adding the hackle and wing using either the full Templedog style or something slimmer. Arctic fox tail hair is the ideal winging material because it is both soft and mobile and long enough to tie flies three inches or more long. Action is the key here, so keep the wing quite long and mobile.

Coloured aluminium cones are the lightest; brass or tungsten versions are heavier. Fluorescent cones are available, too. You don't have to use just one cone – two or more of different colours increase the weight and the range of possible effects.

tip

• Smaller flies incorporating coneheads should be dressed with a sparse wing to maintain mobility.

Mikael Frödin tubes

4 Fold the hair back then fix it in place so that it sits up high over the top of the cone. This forms the base for subsequent layers. Take another, longer, bunch of the hair and catch it in front of the first bunch so that it, too, sits up high. Secure with tight thread turns.

5 Catch in a large, soft-fibred cock hackle and wind on three full turns in front of the wing. Add a second hackle in the same way, stroking the fibres back at each turn so they sit back over the body.

6 Add a few mixed strands of pearl and gold Flashabou. Take a long, slim bunch of Arctic fox tail and fix it securely in place over the top of the two previous layers. Add jungle-cock cheeks then complete the dressing with a small head and whip finish.

Mix and Match

Salmon and sea trout flies in endless variation from a sea-fisherman's tackle bag

A novel system of creating a range of salmon and sea trout flies was initiated by an anonymous contributor to *Trout and Salmon* magazine. He suggested that tiny low-water tube-flies could be tied on the crimps sea-fishermen use to make up wire traces (see tip, page 127). Indeed they can, and these tiny microtubes have proved very successful.

The crimps vary from about 3mm long to nearly 2.5cm and can be made in brass, aluminium or copper. The nickel-silver crimp is useful and effective, and they are also available in matt black. This variety of contrasting finishes prompted a further development. Slim, sinuous flies can be created by mounting two of these slender crimp-flies, one behind the other. The leading one has a trailing hair wing. There is no need to stop at two. Longer versions, combining black and silver crimps, have been thoroughly approved by the sewin of the Towy. Bulkier salmon flies are created by dressing each segment.

There is a danger of the nylon cast fraying where it enters the unlined crimp tube. The solution is to insert the very fine tubing designed for mounting cone heads or the body tube used for fly-tying. Both sorts of tube can have their ends burred with a flame.

The variations of tube length and colour and of the colour, texture and length of wing open up vast possibilities, and there is yet more. You can get more movement into the body by threading beads between the body sections. The tiny beads used to make eyes on trout flies fit beautifully between the crimps: they add very little weight and come in a variety of colours. Gold-head beads and coneheads in various colours can also be slipped into a sequence that, who knows, might prove to be the next Willie Gunn.

Tube-fly materials

By adding crimps, beads and coneheads all sorts of permutations are possible

happy returns

- If you like using tube-flies but practise catch-and-release, or are fishing at a time when you are likely to meet coloured fish, replace the traditional treble hook with a straight-eyed barbless single. Carp hooks are ideal.

Other spec

ies

Almost any fish can be caught on a fly. Fish are omnivorous little devils. A species may show a marked preference for a particular food but they will rarely pass up an easy meal if one is on offer. Even plankton feeders will grab a passing nymph. The salmon eats nothing in fresh water but is caught on the fly.

Roach and rudd can be caught on tiny nymphs and small black midge imitations if your reactions are quick enough. Dace take any small trout fly with lightning speed and chub are regularly caught on all trout flies but are particularly partial to something meaty – a chunky imitation of a beetle or daddy-long-legs. A near-record chub on the River Annan took a salmon fly. Trout fishermen on Corrib and Ullswater can be pestered with perch. Even the slow and suspicious carp can be fooled by a static 'fly' of fluffy white and brown marabou looking for all the world like a bread crust – but only once.

But none of these fish can offer the vim and vigour of the dashing trout, grayling or salmon. To equal that thrill the angler must look for larger quarry, in freshwater and in salt.

Anglers have always taken sea fish with flies. The mackerel feathers jigged from day-trip fishing boats through the summer months are simple but effective flies. The mackerel has little chance to show its paces while trailing a 4oz lead weight, but on a fly rod a mackerel is strong and very fast. Mackerel, alas, seldom come close enough to the shore to be taken on a cast fly, but there is a sporting fish that hunts right into the rocks and breakers. Sea bass are relentless predators, the wolves of the breaking waves.

The pike is the top predator in many fresh waters. It may lack the elan of the bass, but the pike grows much, much bigger.

Both these formidable predators hunt smaller fish and both are willing – eager – to take suitably crafted imitations cast with a fly rod.

Pike

Fly-fishing for a legendary predator

If you go fly-fishing for sport rather than the pot then pike offer an excellent sporting (and cheaper) alternative to game fish – particularly in the winter months. Under the right conditions, pike readily take a fly and there are many waters – running and still – that are infested with pike. Even a small pike of 2–3lb will prove a worthy opponent on light game tackle. There are plenty of waters where pike well into the teens can be taken and that's an experience to test the nerve of any fisherman.

These big fish need big flies. Pike flies are not out-sized trout flies: they are a distinct class of pattern on their own. They have been developed to imitate the pike's prey: other large fish (up to two-thirds the pike's own length), preferably wounded or disabled. Casting such huge flies can test the fisherman and his tackle. They should be tied as light and bulky as possible. Non-absorbent artificial materials and light natural hairs are the prescription. Bucktail is ideal. Tie them on big saltwater fly hooks or

BALLYDOOLAGH BOMBER

HOOK: **Size 3/0 phantom**

THREAD: **Strong white**

TAIL: **Yellow bucktail**

WING: **Orange bucktail with black artificial hair over**

HACKLE: **Dyed-red cock hackle**

HEAD: **Closed cell foam**

TYING THE BALLYDOOLAGH BOMBER

1 Shape a piece of closed cell foam to form the head. Stick it to the hook with superglue. Colour the head and add an eye to each side. Run the tying thread down the shank. Catch a bunch of yellow bucktail a short distance back from the bend.

2 With three or four turns, pull tight: the bucktail will flare around the hook. Add a bunch of orange bucktail with tips level to the tail tips.

3 Bind waste ends with tight turns, creating a secure body. Add an overwing of black crinkle hair, tips level with the tail and wing tips.

4 Select two dyed-red hackles with fibres a little longer than the hook gape. Catch in just behind the foam head. Wind the hackle to form a collar.

5 Secure the hackle tips. Cast off with a whip finish. Run superglue into the base of the hackle and whip finish. A nylon monofilament weed guard is an optional refinement.

RELATED SUBJECTS: • Fish imitations p96 • Fishing with combinations of flies p104

sea hooks. Sizes up to 4/0 or 5/0 are not out of the question. Don't worry: you will be able to cast them on a size 8–9 rod, but you may have to accept a shorter cast when punching out a huge fly and wire trace. The answer may be to fish from a belly boat if the thought of dangling your feet amid large carnivores doesn't disturb you.

John Wilshaw with a 22¼lb pike from Chew Valley Lake

Bass

The latest fashion in fly-fishing has ancient roots

Salt water fly-fishing for bass may be the fastest-growing branch of the sport but it is nothing new around British coasts. JC Wilcocks, in *The Sea Fisherman* gave tips for the taking of bass on the fly: '…they can be taken by rowing windward of the shoal and casting the flies amongst them, drawing the fly quickly through the shoal of fish by short jerks'. That was back in 1868. The method holds true today, nearly one and a half centuries later.

But what fly? The bass that come inshore to forage among the rocks and skerries on a rising tide are hunting the sand eels and herring fry (known as brit) that seek shelter from the perils of the open sea.

Sand eel imitations (see pages 110–111), that are used by the more enterprising of sea-trout fishermen to catch sea trout in coastal waters, work very well, but a shorter pattern of fly, imitating the brit fry of the herring and pilchard that spawn around the coast, may have a broader appeal outside the estuaries.

TRUE BRIT

HOOK: Size 1/0 Mustad 34011 or similar. Hooks should be coated or stainless

THREAD: Strong white

UNDERBODY & WING: Neer Hair (synthetic bucktail substitute)

FLANK SHINER: Pearl Mylar

OVERWING: Pearly purple Angel Hair

BACK: Peacock Angel Hair

HEAD: Epoxy varnish and stick-on holographic eyes

Bass-fishing with the True Brit

RELATED SUBJECT: • Fish imitations p96

tips

- Fish the True Brit on a floating or intermediate line. Deep sinking lines do have their place but, from the beach or among rocks, the sand eel and herring fry you are imitating are more often in the upper layers of water.
- If fishing from the shore, a line tray is an essential piece of equipment. Step on a fly line around a trout fishery and little damage is done: step on a line on a barnacle-covered rock and it could be cut in two.

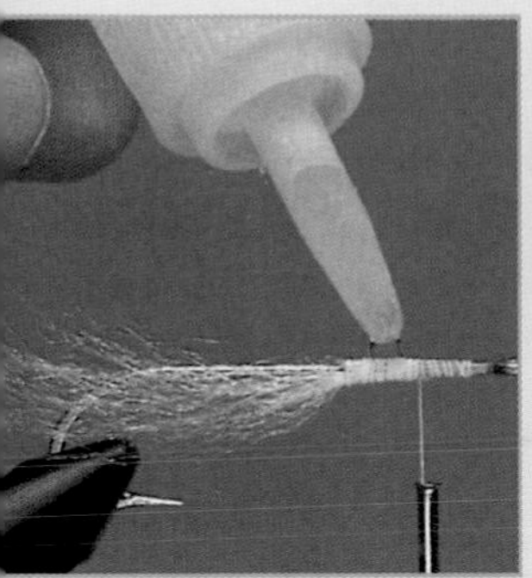

1 Lay down a bed of thick thread for one-third of the shank. Form an underbody 'beard' with a tuft of Neer Hair past the bend of the hook. Add a dab of superglue so that when tying in the overbody wing it is wound into wet glue.

2 Tie in a wing of Neer Hair so that it is almost twice the length of the hook shank. Begin to build the head shape over the wet glue.

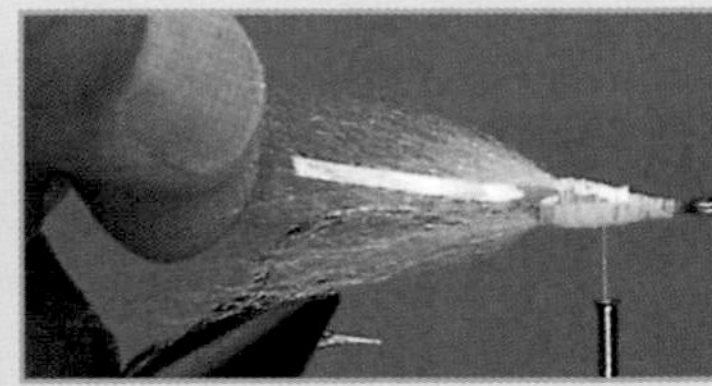

3 Tie in the flank shiner strip from a length of pearl Mylar or similar. This strip reflects along the lateral line and makes a significant difference to the fly's attraction.

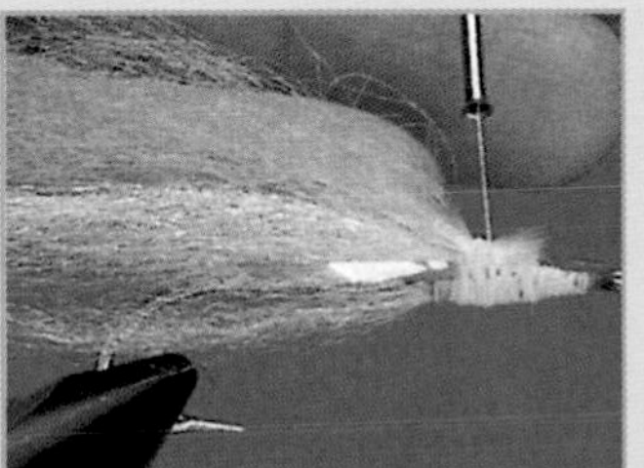

4 Give the head a dab of superglue and tie in a fairly sparse overwing of pearly purple Angel Hair.

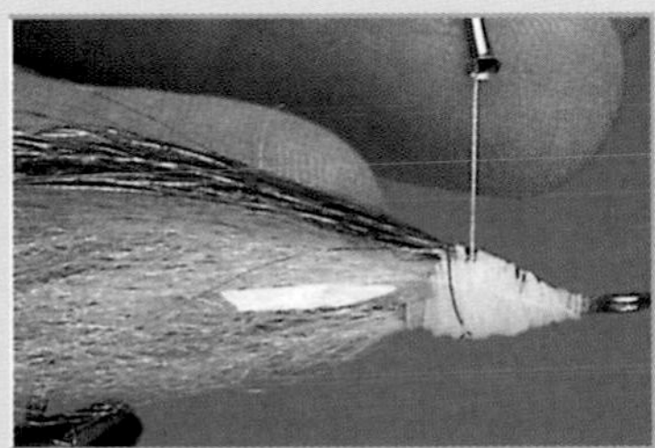

5 Tie in a back of peacock Angel Hair to simulate the back of the herring fry.

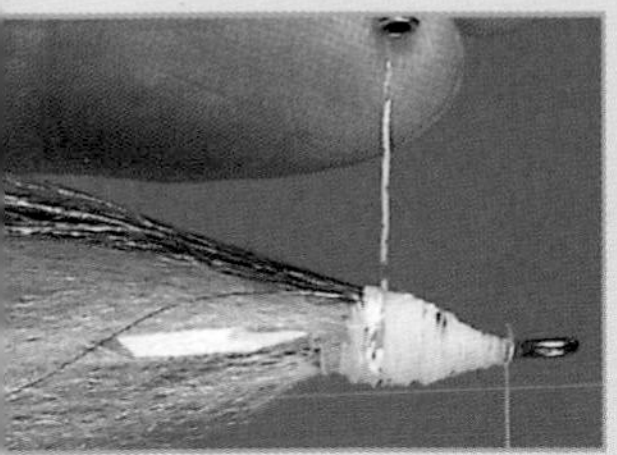

6 The head shape should now be finalized, so tie in a pearly Mylar strip and cover the head shape so that it will glisten and reflect under the epoxy coating.

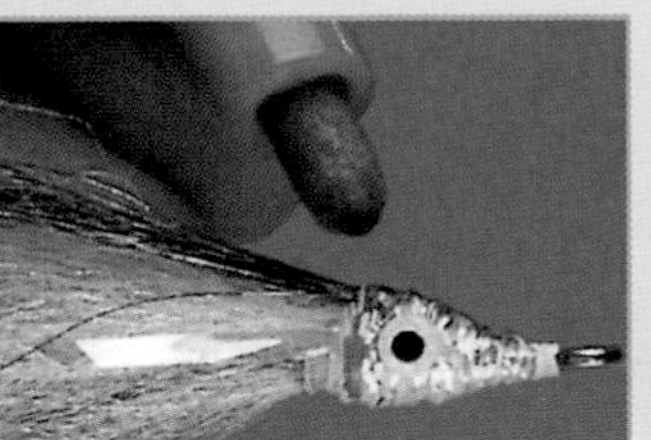

7 Tie off and stick on a 4mm self-adhesive holographic eye to each side of the head. Draw in a representation of the gill cover edges with a red indelible marker pen.

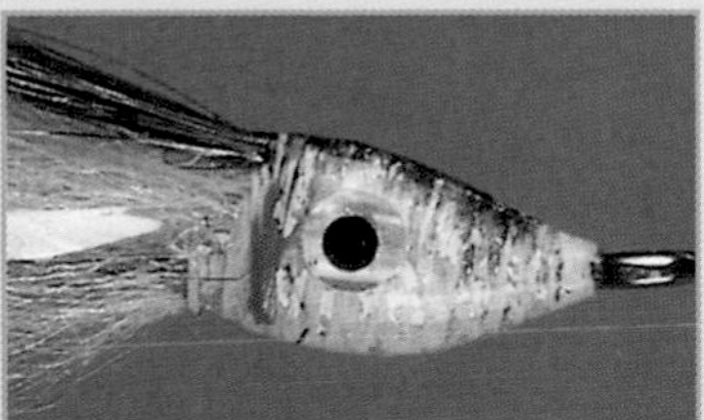

8 Mix up some epoxy and coat the head. Rotate the fly until the epoxy thickens enough to stop running and then leave to dry completely.

To Barb or Not To Barb?

Experts from the world of fly-fishing give their opinion

JOHN HORSEY

Competition fisher and stillwater guide

'While I totally agree with the policy of barbless hooks for trout that are to be released, I simply detest having to use them. Barbless hooks hold fish as well as those with barbs? Forget it!'

MICHAEL EVAN

Vice-president of the Game Angling Instructors Association

'While not a fan of either barbed or pure barbless hooks, I have great faith in those which have had the barb pressed down to leave a bump. Thus treated, their holding powers are the equal of barbed hooks and the salmon can be released quickly and with the minimum of fuss.'

CHARLES JARDINE

Stillwater, stream and saltwater specialist

'I used to be a zealot of the barbless cause, but not any more. I switched to the now popular microbarbed hooks. I was getting fed up with losing trout on stillwaters as a result of fishing barbless flies. Give me a short hook-point and small barb any day. When it comes to releasing a fish from a micro-barb hook, a quick underwater tweak and away it goes.'

MIKE WEAVER

Wild trout fly fisherman

'On a wild fishery you will catch considerable numbers of small fish which must be quickly released with the absolute minimum of damage, making the change to barbless hooks a logical development. The welfare of the fish apart, the lack of a barb is really appreciated when trying to remove a fly from clothing, nets and thumbs.'

EOIN FAIRGRIEVE

Tweed gillie

'I have found no significant difference in the number of fish hooked and lost. By maintaining constant pressure and playing the fish hard, the chances of the fish spitting the hook back are much reduced, as is the salmon's stress.'

PETER O'REILLY

Irish all-rounder and vice-president of the Wild Trout Trust

'I have been using barbless hooks for trout fishing – though not exclusively – for about ten years. The biggest surprise is how well they hold and the ease with which they can be removed.'

GARY LYTTLE

Stillwater and grayling expert

'I use micro-barbed hooks for my stillwater fishing and then remove the barb if I want to catch-and-release. All my river patterns are tied on barbless hooks and I don't have any problems losing fish. Barbed hooks are a thing of the past.'

JONATHAN JONES

Welsh fly fisherman

'It all depends what you are fishing for. I use barbless hooks for all my trout and grayling fishing and cannot say that I lose any more fish than I did before making the change. But no one will ever convince me that sea trout and barbless hooks go together.'

Patenting a fly

You may, one day, stumble across the Holy Grail of the fly-fisherman, the perfect irresistible fly. Will it lead to wealth beyond the dreams of avarice?

Q *I'm a keen fly-tyer and trout fisherman. I've been using my own pattern to great success, so much so that other anglers have offered to buy it. Is it possible to patent a fly pattern? If so, how do I go about doing this?*

A Yes, you can patent a fly, but it's expensive and you've got to be sure that it's worth it.

Ideally the fly should have unique qualities distinguishing it from other patterns. If you've marketed the fly already (sold it to other anglers) the process of patenting becomes almost impossible. It's best to keep quiet about it, get it patented and then market it. Otherwise your pattern is open to copying by other tyers.

So what's the process? You have to contact a company specializing in patenting. They'll demand samples and descriptions of the pattern, including its variants. Full tying instructions must also be provided.

After the patent has been filed you can license a fly-tying company to produce the fly on your behalf.

Glossary

Beard hackle Hackle fibres gathered underneath the hook shank, behind the head of the fly. Also called a *throat* hackle. If formed from a bunch of fibres (rather than wound), it may be called a *false* hackle

Caddis (*see* Sedges). The caddis was originally the larval stage of a sedge fly.

Caenis The smallest of the upwinged flies. They are hard to imitate and thus have earned the name 'Angler's Curse'.

Cape Skin, with feathers attached, from the head and neck of a bird, usually a hen or cockerel.

CDC *see* Cul-de-canard

Cheeks Feathers, usually jungle cock, tied one to each side of a fly, to suggest eyes.

Chironomids The various species of midge of the genus *chironomus*.

Cul-de-canard The buoyant, fluffy feathers from around a duck's preen gland.

Daphnia One family of minute zooplankton that can form a significant part of a trout's diet in lowland stillwaters.

Dapping A form of fly-fishing in which the fly is not cast but carried downwind by the breeze on a length of fluffy *dapping floss*.

Dropper A short length of line branching from the leader to carry an additional fly.

Dub To attach filaments of wool, hair or other fibres (the dubbing) to the tying thread. This is wound up the hook shank to form a dubbed body. Hare's ear fur is a widely used dubbing material.

Dun The penultimate stage of an upwinged fly's lifecycle. The winged dun (or *sub-imago*) hatches from the nymph at the water's surface. Within hours it will transform into the full adult (the *imago* or spinner) to mate, lay eggs and die. Also a colour of hackle feather.

Grilse A salmon returning to the river after spending just one winter at sea.

Hackle (1) The neck feather of a bird, often a cockerel or hen. (2) The turns of such a feather on an artificial fly. These are usually just behind the head but can be wound along the length of the body in a *palmered* hackle. See also beard hackle, throat hackle and parachute hackle.

Herl A fibre attached to the central quill of a feather.

Imago The adult stage of an upwinged fly, also called a spinner.

Leader The length of monofilament line at the end of the flyline.

Mayfly Strictly speaking the name refers (in Britain and Europe) to just two species, the almost identical *Ephemera danica* and *Ephemera vulgata*. In the United States – and increasingly elsewhere – mayfly refers to any upwinged fly of the order *Ephemeroptera*.

Natural The real, living fly (as opposed to the artificial).

Olives A fairly general term for medium-sized upwinged flies. Strictly-speaking, olives are the genus *Baëtis* of the order *Ephemeroptera*.

Palmer (Also palmered and palmer-style) – a type of fly with a hackle wound in open turns along the length of the body

Parachute hackle A hackle wound about a wing or post at right angles to the hook shank. See Klinkhamer Special (page 36) for an example.

Peacock herl The long strands of green or bronze taken from the large tail feathers of a peacock. Usually wound to form a body or thorax.

Point The far end of the leader. The point-fly is at the end of the leader when fishing a team of flies on droppers. Also known as the tail-fly.

PTN Pheasant-tail Nymph

Scissors The angle between the upper and lower jaws of a fish. In a salmon it affords the firmest hook hold.

Sedges Also known as caddis flies, they are aquatic insects with roof-shaped wings of the order *Trichoptera*.

Sewin The Welsh name for sea trout, one of many such local names which include: white trout (Ireland), peal (West Country) and mort (Northwest England).

SLF Synthetic Living Fibre: one of many artificial dubbing fibres sold under a variety of trade names.

Spider Pattern of artificial fly with a simple hackle and no wing.

Spinner The fully mature upwinged fly, usually eaten by trout when trapped, dead or dying, in the water surface.

Stone-flies Aquatic flies of the order *Plecoptera* commonly found in stony rivers.

Sub-imago The *dun* or penultimate stage on an adult upwinged fly.

Tag A short tail, usually of brightly coloured wool or floss, on an artificial fly. It can also be a few turns of silver or gold tinsel at the tip of a salmon fly body.

Throat hackle *see Beard hackle*

Tip Turns of gold or silver tinsel or bright floss at the tail end of fly's body (*see Tag*)

Tippet Golden pheasant tippet. Striking feathers (orange with black bars) from the neck of a golden pheasant. Fibres are used as a tail in many trout flies. The whole feather is used in Ally's and other shrimp patterns.

Topping Golden pheasant topping. Curved yellow feathers from the crest of a golden pheasant. Used as a tail in many flies.

Touching turns The winding of any material along the shank of a hook without leaving gaps or overlapping.

Upwinged flies Aquatic flies of the order *Ephemeroptera.* An alternative name, 'mayflies', can lead to considerable confusion (*see* Mayfly).

Venpol Degreasing agent from Veniards. Other suitable products include Syntrapol and Lux soap flakes.

Whip finish Neat and secure way of finishing the thread turns on a fly. Three half-hitches are a simple alternative.

Index

EDITOR'S THANKS

This book is a distillation of articles and features that have appeared in *Trout and Salmon* magazine, with additional material from *Trout Fisherman*. I would like to thank both publications for their help in compiling the book. I am especially grateful for the unstinting help of Jo Owen and October Ward in unearthing the articles I selected from the archives.

In selecting material, I have relied very heavily on the expertise, wisdom and authority of Peter Gathercole, without whom the book would not have been possible. I am also grateful for the invaluable contributions of Paul Procter, John Roberts, Peter Dunne, Stan Headley, Tom Fort, Davie McPhail, Roy Christie, Crawford Little, John Horsey, Rod Tye, Nick Dunn, Nigel Savage, Tommy Shaw, Bill Cottle, Russel Hill, Russ Symons, Richard Archer, Mike Coleman, Michael Evans, Charles Jardine, Mike Weaver, Eoin Fairgrieve, Peter O'Reilly, Gary Lyttle, Jonathan Jones.

Max Fielding